We were poor, we were black, we had all the strikes already called against us but none of it touched us because we were deep. On Sunday, or whenever it was that all of it was allowed to hang out, no one had to peek over his or her shoulder to see if a "higher" caste member was looking down on us, or if anyone was sneering with disapproval. We were all in the same boat and we knew it.

We belonged to each other and we knew that too. Those of us who constituted the first generation born in the Nawth were not very different from our elders. We weren't offered any new kinds of privileges to any great extent because they couldn't be afforded.

SCARS
AND
MEMORIES

ODIE HAWKINS

Originally published by Holloway House Publishing Co.

Copyright © 1987, 2011 by Odie Hawkins

Front cover photo by Zola Salena-Hawkins,
www.flickr.com/photos/32886903@N02

ISBN: 978-1-5040-3591-0

Distributed in 2016 by Open Road Distribution
180 Maiden Lane
New York, NY 10038
www.openroadmedia.com

To
Iyalosa Tanina Songobumni
With Love

Scars
And
Memories

Chapter 1

As though the brick was caught in midair by a mad ass slow motion process I saw it moving into the middle of my forehead. The dull thud it made in the center of my forehead makes me ache, even now.

Sometimes, when I've been drunk, or doped up, I drift off, seeing, feeling the half of a house brick Junior threw into my skull.

There were other bricks of different kinds but they were never as vivid. I couldn't've been older than seven or eight and I'll never remember what provoked our fight.

My mother was holding my arms to keep me from kicking Junior's ass when the brick came. I know how she felt because it was normally against her nature to be nonviolent.

We were living on 50th and South Parkway (King Drive now) in a basement with Uncle Thomas and Aunt Mamie, my mother, sister, father and sometimes Marthann (and her ol' man) and Aunt Bessie (Marthann's mother).

I don't remember where we all slept but we lived there. I revenged on Junior a few days later. I spotted him, snatched a rope from some girls playing Double Dutch and went hyena on his ass.

I'm sure I gave him a good lashing but the feeling is vague. Just goes to show you how pale revenge can be.

A hole in the center of my head, a lifetime scar, a heavy way to relate to a time zone. But that wasn't all. A guy on a horse with a sword stuck up in the air, on permanent duty, stood across the street from our basement, right in front of the Grand Hotel.

It was years later that I learned that it was a statue of George Washington, slave master. By then I had enough sense to realize that it was an insult to the black community. Memories . . .

The southside was my community. I loved the southside. I loved the westside too. And the northside too, and still do, whenever I think about what they were like.

The memories are so sharply etched that I have to drink wine, snort coke and smoke Indica in order to make certain that some blurring occurs, that way what I'm writing doesn't simply become a report.

Haphazardly, I jumped off the fifth step of the stairs leading down into the basement we lived in at the time and landed squarely on a rat's hind quarters.

Po' rat just happened to be making his move 'round about that time. He squeaked and drug himself away, crippled. I stood there, a two square landing, shook up.

I can see my father and cousin Claude, men who loved each other and life, sitting in a doorway on a humid summer day, flies buzzing around the corners of their cheap wine-sweetened lips. They weren't bums, just drunks for the day, brothers who didn't give a damn.

And running into the car from between two cars, smack

dab into the side door.

Incredible feeling, that daffy feeling you feel, running into the side of a car. You see and hear but you feel too hurt to say anything.

They took me to Henrotin Hospital. I lost my two front teeth but others grew in. I must've been young enough to be starting on my last set.

Memories

So much was happening so fast at times. I'd be living on the northside, in Uncle Eddie's basement (jumping onto rat backs) and then suddenly, I'd be living in Aunt Mary's basement on the westside.

Washburne Avenue, from Racine on the western border and Blue Island (Blue   Island?) on the eastern border, was one of the streets I got to know in a way that I've never known any other place.

It seems, in some ways, that I became totally aware of where I was, on Washburne. (I may say the same thing about the Almo Hotel, or the Avon, when I get to them.) It (Washburne) was a small town with realistic people.

On the south side of the street, at the corner, was a Jewish owned grocery store. A brother who worked there had learned how to speak Yiddish. The memory of him reminding one of his employers (who had been speaking Yiddish to someone else) that he had something else to do on that particular day sticks/stuck in my mind.

This Black man (boy, actually) had understood what these people were saying in this weird language. Fantastic.

Next door to the grocery store was this bus that someone had converted into a candy store/notions parlor.

It was the place to buy your penny candy. Funny, no one ever thought of it as a converted bus.

Next to that, going east, was Mrs. Richardson's beauty shoppe. Varnette Honeywood does Mrs. Richardson's beauty shoppe to artistic perfection.

I can close my eyes and see women (my Aunt and other ladies getting their hair done) squirming slightly as the hot combs probed the "kitchens." I can't recall the reasons for me being on the scene, but I was there.

A narrow passageway and a window leading down into a basement where an old man sold coal through his front basement window.

We called him Mr. Something or other. He had a peculiar status based on coal. Which meant, if you ran out of coal in the middle of the winter, he could be your saviour. A primeval coke dealer in a manner of speaking.

I see Moochie and Edna and Tweet in Aunt Mary's basement. My sister and I, Aunt Mary, Uncle Percy, Uncle Eddie (my father sometimes) and maybe two or three other guests—people who'd hung onto the cards or dice too long.

The rats used to sleep with us in this basement. We knew they had slept next to our warm bodies the next morning because we would find their prints beside our bodies and their little tight black droppings. And sometimes we would know they were there because they crawled over our bodies. Terrible place, that basement at 1150 West Washburne Avenue. Terrible. But the vibes were good.

Across the street, on the first floor, was a couple or a trio of teenaged girls, friends of my cousins, one of them introduced me to Spanish. The book was titled *El Camino Real* and I think she was astounded to discover that I could get off on "El burro no es inteligente."

"You came a long way from St. Louie . . ." a piece of music for the time slithers through my consciousness.

The dances were very African then, the boys danced and the girls danced back, holding on for dear cultural life, with rhythmic blossoms stirring them on.

Underneath the first floor of this building was a gambling

house called "The Hole." It looked and smelled like a hole too.

Nasty, filth-ridden street, filled with joy. We all knew each other and there was an order to life.

A passageway between the "Hole" and the stone building next to it. Funny building, what I recall about it most is that it was a pale grey brick and felt supercool to the body on a hot day.

Next door was the building where O' Quincy and his sister Bernice lived. There were quite a few others in their family but I can't remember their names.

I remember O' Quincy because he dared me to walk into a bat he was swinging, 'round 'n 'round, one evening. In a classic case of misunderstood signals, I walked into the swinging bat and fell to the ground with a battered right knee. It hurt for years, and may hurt some more.

O' Quincy's sister Bernice, high on religion one fall evening, once hugged me in front of a bunch of people standing around in front of the Sunrise Baptist Church.

She was wearing some kind of fur (rabbit?) and I tripped on the warmth of her embrace. Being young and stupid I simply relaxed and stood there.

Around the corner, on the side of O' Quincy's building was a row of "apartments" that looked like dens. Or caves that had been converted into bunkers.

A beautiful girl, blue-black skinned with porcelain white teeth, lived in one of the bunkers. They had formerly been stables and the smell of hay and manure was always on the air.

The beautiful Black girl's name was Honey and everybody loved her because she was so beautiful. They were very poor, Honey's family. I didn't realize how poor until I popped in to pick up one of her brothers on the way to school and found them eating their cornflakes with water.

A vacant lot where we sometimes played jive ass baseball.

Vacant lot filled with glass, rusty nails, cast off bricks, dead cats 'n rats, whatever gravitated to the ground. It's a wonder we didn't kill ourselves on all that shit. It was worse than the lot behind the Bowen Hotel on Bowen Avenue.

It stimulated a rare passion, this daily romance with the ugly side of life. And yes, it was ugly. The dregs place was what it was, but we didn't recognize that, taking refuge in survival games.

House next to the lot contained a lady who was so fat that she hadn't ventured beyond her front room window for years. When she died the firemen had to chop the doorway away to make room for her final exit. Real big woman, real big.

Something skips past my consciousness and then we get to an alley, and across the cobblestoned alley is a junkyard.

The junkyard sticks in my mind because someone once shot a rat that was as big as a full grown 'possum. I saw it.

Crossing over to the other side of the street, the north side of the street. The northeast corner, to be exact. A supermarket. An A & P (whatever that meant) with an airplane propeller oozing 'round in the ceiling and fragrant aroma of Maxwell House coffee being stirred around.

It was different from the Jewish mom 'n poppa store across the street, more rigid, no credit. Right next to the "supermarket" was a house on stilts.

I think the people who lived in the house on stilts was the poorest family on our street, like they were absolutely poor. Their "house" was made of wooden planks, badly joined. Some of the older, taller boys used to stand underneath the house and look up through the floor boards.

If we (the neighborhood rascals) happened to be up late, roaming around, we might ease the back door of their house open (there was no lock) and peek in at the sleeping bodies scattered around on the pallets.

Dicky was my friend from this household. He couldn't talk

normally for some reason. He made sounds that I understood and he was not shy about yelling 'n squeaking his opinions.

In recent years I've connected a big plastered out spot on his skull with his inability to speak. The rumor was that he had been hit in the head with a ball-peen hammer.

I don't know what the deal was, we were friends and had a lot to say to each other.

Lubertha, his oldest sister, sometimes spent the night with the coalman. The next day her brothers would lug four, sometimes five bushels of coal across the street. A real case of tit for tat.

Everybody knew everything about everybody else on Wash burne. There were no secrets on Washburne.

"Butterbeans" was Dicky's oldest brother. He had beautiful white, buck teeth, kept his fingernails filed and super clean—and hated his nickname. Couldn't blame him really, who the hell wants to be called "Butterbeans"?

I didn't know his middle sister's name but I opened the door one night (just roamin' around) and there she was, on a blanket with her dress hiked up over her hips. A lush, moving sight by oil lamp.

I never really related to her but I was forever fascinated by the fact that I had seen her pussy. It formed an interesting relationship, her lack of knowledge of my knowledge of her.

Next to the house on stilts there was a three story red brick building. The place rests on my head because it's where I saw my first dead person.

There was this old man who lived in the basement, surrounded by slabs of newspapers, who had died. When I stared past the elbows of the adults he seemed to be laying on a slab of newspapers. Coldblooded basement.

Next to the brick was 1150 West Washburne, the basement home of Mrs. Mary Fant alias Aunt Mary alias whatever she had chosen to call herself.

15

Quiet as it was kept, 1150 West Washburne was where it was! We had the charisma! We had the glamor! We had the cards and dice!

The action would begin to happen on Thursday. 1150 West Washburne basement. Two ways to get in and out.

The front way was down some stone steps that took you below the street level.

The front door faced the coal bin where my aunt usually kept five or six dogs (depending on whether it was before or after puppies had been born ... then there might be fifteen or twenty). Most people used the rear entrance.

Rear entrance; down ten steps leading to the alley, through a narrow brick passageway (real cool in the summer) to the doorway on the left after fifteen paces or so.

In the back of my mind the rear entrance to Aunt Mary's (somehow Uncle Percy just never received as much attention, despite the fact that he had once killed a man and served eleven years in Leavenworth) was the essence of what crummy alum living was about.

At night, with no light in the passageway, it was black-black-black. Dark black. To the immediate right of the entrance was where the garbage was kept in a couple bushel baskets (also used for coal) and, inside the baskets underneath the garbage there were rats.

In the summer, if you were bold enough to kick the baskets or throw ashes from the coal stove on them, they would waddle up from the bottom of the baskets, loaded on watermelon rinds, corn on the cob and whatever made them fat, irritated enough to bite the disturbance. In the winter they were always hungry and irritated and best left alone.

The toilet was a few steps beyond the garbage baskets. The toilet was a nightmare space. The door hung on one hinge, the toilet seat was cracked in a few places, the area around the stool trashed over with scraps of one kind or another.

The place staek and, overhead, where the first floor toilet was situated, the ceiling was rotted out, dripping toilet stool water on your head.

At times, the rats, more robust in their play than at other times, would fall through the ceiling. A big one fell on the back of my neck one day, bounced to the floor and stood staring at me for a moment, as though making a decision as to whether or not he wanted a piece of me.

A decision was reached in my favor, he finally wandered off to rejoin the game.

We didn't have to talk about rats, they were a fact of life There was nothing we could do about them. Living the way we did, underground, meant that we were on their turf, in a manner of speaking.

They were too wise to go for poisons or traps and, in addition, there were so damned many of them it would've been a wasted effort to kill a few at a time. We were at the mercy of the rats.

The slumlord? Never laid eyes on him.

Knock! Knock! and the proper verbal identification was sufficient for admission.

It was the kitchen diningroom all purpose space you strolled into. A potbellied coal stove in the middle of the space. Two bedrooms on the north wall of the space with a pantry in between (where Aunt Mary kept her chickens I wrung their necks and slit their throats for many a Sunday dinner).

Pull the curtain back and there was the front room. The front room had a bed off to one side. And a fold out bed stacked against the closet door. (I opened this closet door once, curious because it was the only part of the house I'd never seen. I peeked in on a startled mother rat and her ratlings. I quickly closed the door and never opened it again. The ratlings did not look cute to me.)

When bedtime came, Uncle Percy would unfold the fold ·

ing bed and create more sleeping space (for whoever needed it) by placing planks on milk crates and a mattress on top. Man was a bed making genius.

My two girl cousins were teenagers, nubile, beautiful. Edna was dark and had the look of a Tutsi princess. Moochie was light snuff colored and looked Ethiopian, complete with a semi-Semitic nose.

I loved Moochie and when she got married and moved away I understood what heartbreak was about, especially the kind you can't talk to anyone about.

A bunch of things happened in that basement but that was a biggie for me. I'll come back to the basement later.

Next door was what I now think of as the "Pit." There was this metal pole/tight rope running from the sidewalk to the house in a front yard that was below the street.

Odd situation, the whole street, architecturally. Anyway the big game was to crawl over the wall and do a high wire act the length of the pole and back.

What made it exciting was this crazed, medium sized dog who lunged up at your body like a small crocodile, trying to disturb your balance.

Over the years, having caught a few unbalanced asses he was neurotic enough to know that he might scare you into slipping if he snapped and lunged enough. The dog was really insane but I don't know what was wrong with us.

Odd, I think, years later, how many "refreshment" points we kids had around the neighborhood. No wonder our teeth were in such sad shape.

The neighborhood was laced with passageways. Some led from the street to the alley, some led to other passageways, some of them led nowhere. The passageway between the candy store and Reverend A.T. Tilly's Sunrise Baptist Church was an incredible place, spiritually, emotionally, communally. A basement where church supper and social events were staged. Four, five steps upstairs and you were in the church proper. The stairs leading up to Reverend Tilly's home slanted over the rear section of the church, an aisle fed worshippers to the altar, the choir areas and the heat of the pot bellied stove.

The congregation was devout but real. My Aunt was a deaconess as well as the lady who ran the gambling house a couple houses away. Uncle Percy was also a deacon.

We went to church because we wanted to.

I couldn't imagine more than seventy-five people sitting inside, fully packed. The church was kinda tacky, with worn carpeting and the need for plaster here and there, but it was deep.

Reverend Tilly was (and is, if he is still living) one of the most electrifying speakers I've ever heard. He held me, and quite a few other people, spellbound for many a Sunday. If he had been a bullfighter he would have been from one of the pure schools of feeling, a Manolete or a Carlos Arruza.

He preached from his heart, from his gut, from life. Sometimes he would ask the congregation to give his family some beans or whatever they could afford because he had a wife and children and he was not rich. I can see him now, a small, bullnecked man with thick glasses and a sidewall hair cut, sitting on the steps of the church, in shirtsleeves and suspenders, just talking to his neighbors.

His sermons were full of African-American nuances and poetry, that used the Bible as a reference point. His roaring, whispering and lovely gestures made me feel that I was watching a great actor. And the singing and the soulfullness. I thank the Orisa that I came alone before integration made such a watery situation out of black religious feelings.

Chapter 2

We were poor, we were black, we had all the strikes already called against us but none of it touched us because we were deep. On Sunday, or whenever it was that all of it was allowed to hang out, no one had to peek over his or her shoulder to see if a "higher" caste member was looking down on us, or if anyone was sneering with disapproval. We were all in the same boat and we knew it.

We belonged to each other and we knew that too. Those of us who constituted the first generation born in the Nawth were not very different from our elders. We weren't offered any new kinds of privileges to any great extent because they couldn't be afforded.

Washburne was a small southern town with the north all around it, somewhere. I didn't know where. On a clear day I could see the buildings "downtown' but I didn't really know where it was.

21

Passageway next to the church led to a small dirt yard where we shot marbles a lot. A small, crinkled up old lady with gray hair that fanned out like a small umbrella on her head lived in a basement that resembled a World War I bunker. Can't remember her name but I remember her running out of the house one sunny afternoon screaming, "Roos'velt is dead! Roos'velt is dead!" tears coursing through the erosions in her cheeks, "I just heard it on the radio!"

A vacant lot filed with crap and a fire hydrant in front of it. Firemen from around the corner on Roosevelt Road used to come and open the hydrant for the children on really hot days and we'd get all wet and goofy with the cold water gushing out on us.

George lived in the house next to the vacant lot. George was a German shepherd with one of the most intelligent approaches to biting I've ever known. He wasn't much out front but if you happened to have to pass *his* section of the alley, he would pull an ambush on you.

Sometimes he would stalk you, other times he would just sit up straight and click his ears up a notch, growling softly, as though he were making up his mind as to where he was going to make his mark.

The next few houses are vague. They were there and people I know lived in them but they are not memorable.

In the summer, when the walls of the houses cast off heat waves, we played in the streets. We ran races and I used to win a lot, I was fast.

We played "Ringo Livio!" We played "Sunk the leader!" We played everything we could play, we would've played Pac-Man if he had been on the scene.

We younger ones would watch the older ones, learning what the deal was. Sometimes we didn't go inside 'til two or three o'clock, when the breezes from the lake had cooled things off.

I'd be up the next day, early, hustling. We all hustled. I

would walk over to the South Water Market and pick up cabbages, tomatoes and other stuff that the men who loaded the trucks had dropped. There was one problem with retrieving some of the trash-veggies. Some of the rats in the area were profoundly aggressive.

One summer I got the notion to chop up enough wood to last all winter. I don't know where the notion came from but it grabbed me and turned me into a wood chopping maniac. I went around gathering up wire-slatted crates. I think my supply must've lasted for a couple weeks during a colder than usual September but I still remember how good it felt to see one of my crates pulled in and the fire fed from it.

Memories

I liked being alone, it gave me a chance to rest my head, to think.

I would walk with my dog Dukes, a fierce, fierce little black guy who appeared to be a cross between a giant Chihuahua and a small demon. Shiny black and terrible. He would attack anything or anybody. And he didn't like white people. I don't know how that feeling came about but it was a fact.

We would walk west through the alley running parallel (east and west) to Roosevelt Road—where the Joy Theatre was. That alley was one of the greatest schools I ever attended.

The garbage told me everything. I guess I was a garbageologist without a degree.

I don't think that garbage was picked up more often than every two weeks, not in this particular alley anyway. Seems to me that there was a large mound of stuff in the summer and in the winter, after the first beautiful, lace network snowfall, a small mountain. Many small mountains of stuff in the alley. It could've been a Switzerland in the ghetto.

In the summer I strolled along, stout stick in hand usually, an alley tourist, my trusty companion Dukes sniffing at foreign piss stains and chasing cats who didn't realize that he

23

was their personal, natural-bone enemy.

I picked up used condoms filled with day old semen, studied diaries in Italian (I found out later), puzzled through pages of Hebrew-Yiddish news, watched cats making weird love (before Dukes made his charge), watched human beings suck and lick on each other (black folks were not supposed to be doing those things, back then) through alley-way windows.

Writer-like, I saw myself looking at myself looking at me and wondered about myself. Or him, I should say.

I really couldn't put me together. Why did I seem to be so different from the people around me? The same, but different. It was a question they asked a lot too. I know because I heard them.

I couldn't explain the urge to be in the alley except to inform myself that it was totally interesting. Every garbage heap was a supermarket garage sale college course to me.

And finally, if I had cashed enough bottles and done whatever was necessary to have the fare, I'd wind up at the Joy Theatre for cowboy flicks (Lash LaRue and Bill Starrett or maybe Louis Jordan/not Jourdan). Or the Broadway, half a block down the street.

The movies were better than the garbage piles; not much better, in retrospect, but more colorful and with fewer flies.

Strangely, I knew something was wrong but I couldn't really pin it down. What was happening that was "off" in the movies was what I couldn't pin down.

Number one, ninety-nine percent of what I saw and watched had nothing to do with me, or my lifestyle. The whites on the screen were figures to be looked at, the story to be followed.

I felt no relationship to them. And when they did have a Mantan Moreland bucking his eyes and bumbling through a Charlie Chan number, I felt nothing for that either.

At times, since this was during that incredible era during which black movies were being distributed, I found something of interest happening in a movie featuring "Moms" Mabley, Louis Jordan (playing a cowboy with his slicked down hair) or some other people that I felt something for.

We were really fouled up in those days (probably not more so than now, but in a different way) on the image level. I recall the silhouetted images of people stumbling out of the Broadway (showing *King Soloman's Mines*) muttering obscenities because they felt insulted by the images of the tall African people on the screen.

They were insulted by the sight of these regal black people and rushed home to listen to Amos 'n Andy, played by two white guys. Crazy, I thought. Real crazy.

The movies, as racist as they were, did give me a chance to ignore reality for an hour or so. I could trip inside the movie. house and, despite the bedlam-decibel-noise level, the popcorn boxes wizzing around in front of the screen, the casual fist fights ("What?! you gon' kick whose ass?!") and all the rest ("was that a rat running across the stage?"). I could lose myself in whatever was happening up there.

I can still do it.

The alleys, the movies, hustlin' nickels and dimes, roaming around. That was a big section of the summer.

There was an odd, exotic quality about the summer. Half the time I felt as though I were part of a really strange dream. It could've been because I was so sleepy so much of the time. Going to bed at one or two in the morning, and getting up at seven or eight a.m. is not exactly conducive to having a well rested body. And then, the all night gambling sessions on the weekends.

The dreaminess of things stemmed from other sources too. I often had the feeling of being able to romanticize on the spot, to say to myself, "one day I'll think back on this whole scene and smile." Or laugh. Or cry my eyes out.

Winter was cruel to us. Summer was hot and humid but winter was cruel. Winter made us chapped, ashy, grey, cold. A fire had to be made in the stove, water heated in basins and tubs. A full fledged bath required a maximum effort of will. We were clean but it cost a lot of goose pimples.

Smyth school. I had transferred from somewhere (I've lost track of the number of grammar schools I went to, something like seventeen or eighteen) and wound up in the fourth grade.

One of my teachers' name was Di Florio; she wore her hair in a Brunhilde type rope coil in the back and seemed immensely depressed, despite her energetic concern with our education.

Another teacher, a big bellied, pasty-faced white guy, sticks in my mind because he would, from time to time, slap one of us boys in the face.

I was a good student and gave him no cause to slap me, I'm pleased to say, for his sake. If he had slapped me and I told my family about it they would've done something real primitive, like kill the son of a bitch.

We were capable of it. Moochie and Edna had been kicked out of school the semester before I got there, having threatened a teacher with a straight razor.

I liked school but I could never really seem to figure out what was going on. I could read and make sense of what I read but I couldn't figure out the why of how things were done. At least school was warm and I didn't have to put coal in the stove or take ashes out.

Reading was better than the movies, and you didn't have to dodge flattened popcorn boxes wizzing past your head. Reading is one of the few self defense tools I can actually trace.

One evening, after a walk through Jewtown, my feet and

hands freezing from a stiff winter's cold snap, I popped into the hallway of the Maxwell Street Y.

I'd passed the building a thousand times but never thought about going inside. I thought, haphazardly, that it was connected to the police station around the corner. On this day I went inside.

The warmth of a vestibule on a cold day in Chicago has to be felt to be understood. I stood there, thawing out, thinking of the last few blocks I had to make to the pad.

The sound of somebody playing the piano in one of the upstairs rooms drew me. I was curious, I wanted to know who was playing, "Dream girl, dream girl, awaken to me . . ."

The third door I peeked into was the entrance to the library. I freaked out. Books, books, from the floor to the ceiling. No one on the scene. I started trying to read two or three at the same time.

I finally settled into something about Gypsies and Lawrence of Arabia. I read half of each book while this terribly romantic music was drifting through the hallways.

Now I really had an educational program going on. I was soaking up the homebrewed stuff, (story tellin' 'n life situations) the beautiful church stuff (thank you, Reverend Tilly), stuff I found in the alley, (I must have handled every germ known, at one time or another, poking around in the garbage piles) Jewtown and the library.

Jewtown. That's exactly what it was, the place where the Jews lived and worked.

On the near westside, during the time this scene was happening, in the area called Jewtown, there were Jews.

I didn't think of them as being victims of persecution. I didn't think of their religion. I didn't think of them as an economic element in our community, which they were. I really didn't think of them or know very much about them.

To me, strolling through the outdoor stalls piled with all

kinds of stuff, they were a funny bunch of men and women who talked funny and were always trying to coax you into going home to get your mother, to have her come back and buy you a pair of shoes or something. Or if your mother was with you, it saved time.

I didn't know what they were doing. I didn't really know anything about buying and selling, or capitalism or Judaism. I just thought they were kind of funny, if anything.

The Gypsies I took seriously. Maybe it had something to do with the book I'd stumbled across in the library. Or the fact that I understood the nomadic life. Whatever it was that helped to understand them existed in me.

The Gypsies lived in a cluster of store fronts at the end of Jewtown. They were totally improbable neighbors. The hard working Jewish salesmen standing in front of their stalls in sub-zero weather, trying to make a buck, and the Gypsies who didn't seem to give a damn about anything materialistic.

These were authentic Gypsies who spoke their own language and always made me think of open spaces and wild birds.

They made a lasting impression on me, this contrast between people. The Gypsies were freer. I had a suspicion, when I saw their children running across the streets, in the winter, half naked, that they were paying a helluva price for their freedom but it still seemed better than standing in front of a stall all day, trying to sell factory irregulars for a nickel profit.

Gypsies, nomads, memories.

Chapter 3

We were like Gypsies, my mother, my sister and me. We were always moving. As I write this. I have to stumble back and forth between the northside, (that's clear, we only lived in my Uncle Eddie's basement on the northside) the southside and the westside. The lake forms the eastside in Chicago and I can almost say we lived on the eastside, that's how close we came to the lake.

Another basement. This one belonged to the Doty family. The Dotys. Mr. Doty worked all the time. I see a vague, dark figure in overalls. That's Mr. Doty. Mrs. Doty often spoke to my mother about having once won a beauty contest. The lady did have spectacular dimensions, not flamboyant but there   38-24-38 or something like that.

The Dotys may have been a young couple but they seemed old to me and my sister.

And then there were the two Doty children and their grandmother, an old Indian woman who sewed beautiful designs on different things all the time.

My sister and I were slightly older than the Doty children and immensely more sophisticated, after all, we had been around the city.

The Doty boy was a six year old (or was he four?) prick and a brat. Mean lil' son of a bitch who kept the household semi-terrorized. My outstanding memory of our time in their basement rests on the time that I poured a bowl of soup on the lil' asshole's head. He wasn't autistic or anything, just mean 'n evil. Maybe he had experienced a bad birth or something.

A short time afterwards we moved down the street to the Almo Hotel, 3800 Lake Park Avenue. Maybe my soup action was the catalyst.

Quite a few Japanese lived on Lake Park then. I see them laughing and talking in front of their apartments down the street from the hotel, but I really had no idea who they were or how they had gotten there (my study of Japanese-American history was still 'way ahead).

In school, Oakenwald, there were always Japanese (Misaki Mishamora, the Fujiwaras, the round faced girl that I loved, Joan Sunahara, Ernest Higa) and whites. Integration was in full swing without anybody really knowing about it, or so it seemed.

The Almo Hotel was, no doubt in my head, the vanguard of a decadent movement, the plunge of a neighborhood into a slum. It didn't take a million years to accomplish the deed.

The Almo Hotel, 3800 Lake Park Avenue. Memories, scars. A four story brick, reddish colored building with slabs of concrete steps that people sat on from morning to morning. Real cool in the summer.

Slum building, grim, glum, run down, even then. Whores used the building for their trade (first floor, part of the second floor). We lived on the third floor in the rear at one point, and then on the south side of the building, facing the vacant lot. We seemed to move around a lot even when we were stationary, my mother, my sister and I.

A family spot, the Almo. My Aunt Mamie and Uncle Thomas lived on the second floor in the rear and my Aunt Bessie lived in the building, from time to time. It was one of those places designed to cope with transients.

Everything happened in the Almo, everything. Sometimes the young bloods of the neighborhood, hostilities surfacing, would put on a rolled up newspaper head whuppin' session down in the basement.

The idea behind this savagery was to see who would scream. Or cry. Or call it quits. I don't know what it's like now but the Chicago Tribune was like a cherrywood baton in those days. And the Times wasn't a bit softer.

As the perpetually "new dude" on the block I had to have my head beaten a few times. It really didn't matter if you won because that simply entitled you to meet another challenger. By the time you got to the third head your newspaper-club would be frayed to pieces, which meant that you were fighting with a fucked up club.

It was a brutal, stupid game that had one cold blooded purpose, to weed out the weaklings. If you broke down and cried, you were degraded forever and given the title "crybaby." If you crumbled and tried to shield yourself you'd be considered a lifelong coward. You couldn't do anything under the circumstances but hit back, even with a frayed newspaper.

There was a grocery store in the basement too, owned by a family named Rich. The Rich's made a fantastic sausage in a number ten tub, packaged it and called it "Rich's Country Style Sausage." They got fairly wealthy from sausage sales at one time and had their own factory, went a long way from the number ten tub. Good sausage.

The winos drank, the dope fiends shot dope, the 'hoes

hoed, the good people did their good square number and we all coexisted, more or less peacefully.

It was life at the most precarious. Anything could happen at any time. A bilked trick could put in a reappearance with a machine gun. Or somebody would nut out and often did. Lots of tensions existed and lots of love. Life was sensationally chancy but there was always tomorrow, or so we deluded ourselves into believing.

Strange, I just suddenly recalled that this was the second time I had lived in the Almo. The first time was when I was younger, going to Oakenwald School and the second time was when I started high school.

I'm talking about the second time, right in through here.

I had my first daughter in the Almo. Strange, how it happened. But probably no stranger than anything else that was happening at that point in life.

Her name was Clara and in today's slinky model factories, she would've been a Givenchy star. It started innocently enough, our number; I felt sorry for her.

Her parents were Almo Hotel-run-of-the-mill winos who neglected her, didn't talk to her, so far as I could tell, and never thought about telling her that they loved her.

I took her emotionally into the twilight zone by bringing her ice cream from Carnegie Drugstore on the Gold Coast, in the Drake Hotel.

My delivery "boy" job allowed me the opportunity to make generous tips delivering drugs to rich old females and steal quarts of exotic ice cream. Peach melba, French vanilla, German whup whip, Mexican slush and such stuff offered me a power laden leverage for the sister's charms. They didn't have any ice cream in those flavors in our neighborhood. We kissed. Memories.

She lay underneath me, the first time, on the floor of a fourth floor toilet, a brilliant white moon shining down on our feverish activities. I didn't love her and I was doing what I was doing because no one seemed to care for her. Girl was so tall 'n skinny. The only way we could do anything was to stretch out side by side. Poor girl.

I was lustful, dumb and a bunch of other good things but she was poor. Poverty stricken in the worse way, she was unloved.

It was simple, almost stupid. In a front room, rented by my Aunt Bessie for a time, we squirmed and scuffled ourselves into the classic missionary position.

Hot, humid, juicy Chicago night, the voices on the stabbed steps below release frequent soft gales of laughter, a bit of heavy cussin'   "awww fuck you in your nose, motherfucker!"

Somebody passing a bottle of wine around, or several people sharing a quart of beer. Any way to get the daily alcoholic fix.

She kept asking me, again and again, "Do you love me?! do you love me?! do you love me?!"

I exploded and finally said, "Yeah, yeah, I luv you, okay?"

A fierce grind on her thin model's pelvic area, a volcanic explosion and a sneaky exit. Love?

I was so stupid that I didn't really connect her belly bloating up with what we had done. I knew that women had babies from having sex but Clara and I? Me 'n Clara? Nawwww, just couldn't be.

The people in the building thought it was cute, going around speculating on what the little crumbcrusher would look like. A baby? Me 'n Clara? Naw, couldn't see it in a million years.

Nevertheless, she returned from the hospital one afternoon, a statistic on the chart of Black females (under sixteen) who had given birth that year.

Me? With some kind of perverted-supershy-perverse machismo going for me, I decided not to see the baby. I don't know why I didn't want to see the baby. I still don't.

Clara, the baby and her mother moved soon after. I didn't

see her again for a few years and by then she had become mean, bitchy, crazed. Naturally.

My daughter, Carmen, at five, was already becoming tall and skinny. Consumptive.

At this stage of the game I began to pay some attention to patterns and what was happening to my life, not just my sex life.

I suspect that working in the drugstore had something to do with opening my eyes, just a trifle.

I found the Gold Coast lifestyle incredible. It was truly incredible, coming from where I was coming from.

Here I was, going back and forth to Lake Shore Drive every other day (I worked part time), where people had everything to where people didn't even have the basic necessities.

I wasn't awed by the magnificence of the huge, glittering kitchens (delivery boys went to the back door) or by the occasional peek I managed of the walnut paneled dining rooms. What I was, more than anything, was real fuckin' pissed off because they had so much and we had so little. Needless to say, I've been even more annoyed ever since then.

Going back, memories.

Moving. The Bowen Hotel on Bowen Avenue, which wasn't really a hotel at all. In the basement again. This one unlike some others that I had experienced, was like being in some kind of hell.

Nice brick shell on the building, steps that were almost like the entrance to a small museum, facaded by those big stone slabs that were so cool to sit on in the summer.

I think we must've been wandering through a poorer than usual period to have wound up down there.

The descent was made from a terrazo tiled lobby; the building must have been a choice place at one time, down through a wooden door to a winding wooden staircase. Dim light bulb. Or none at all.

Through three yards of dim hallway. To the right was a toilet stool and a bathtub, with some planks loosely nailed around the "facilities." It resembled an outdoor toilet, indoors. The people in the front apartment entered and exited through their front door on the street. The rest of us came and went down the dim steps.

What it really was, was this; after a basement fire (I smelled the smoke from the day we moved in until years afterwards) an enterprising slumlord had decided to rent plasterboard cubicles out. He could have turned some kleenex boxes upside down and achieved the same effect.

Miserable fuckin' place, miserable. Each cubicle had three plywood sides and a stone back wall. The back wall was runny, like an old fashioned dungeon. In the summer everything that lived underground crawled out of the wall, and it wasn't too much better in the winter.

A beautiful old lady named Miz Whitehead lived in the next cubicle, she and I don't know how many other Whiteheads. Week after week they kept coming. From somewhere in deepest Miss'sippi, I think. Next cubicle, a small, yellowish-skinned woman who was always pregnant and having miscarriages. And at the end of the cubicle strand, Jean and her baby, Henry Jr.

We shared a two burner in the middle of a kitchen that had once been the building's laundry room. The cement on the floor had potholes, we got our water from the two faucets above the cement rinse basins.

Roaches congregated by the hundreds on the wall above the basins as soon as the light in the kitchen was turned off. And sometimes before it was turned off.

Roaches, junkies, memories. The roaches were everywhere, in your clothes, in your shoes, everywhere. The junkies occupied a more limited space. The gentlemen's agreement we had with them permitted them to sit down, sleep, shoot dope or whatever, after most of us had gone to bed.

35

It was a workable arrangement, one that bought us the first choice of porterhouse steaks and whatever else the junkies might rip off. And, as anybody with junkie-knowledge knows, they will steal sweetness out of gingerbread.

They weren't bad guys basically, just junkies who would've murdered us in our sleep if they thought it would get them more dope.

I saw them shoot dope, wandering out of my room to go to the toilet. Or to play a midnight game I called "killin' the roaches." What I'd do was roll a newspaper into a cone and start slowly burning the bottom ranks clustered on the damp wall above the kitchen sink or above the tub in the toilet.

Sometimes I'd manage to go through two or three ranks before they fully realized what was happening and begin scattering.

Revenge was extremely sweet. Memories

Like I said, I don't really know why we were so exceptionally poor in the basement. Maybe the stocks had plunged to a new low or something. There was a chronic lack of food, few decent garments, lots of desperate moves. I wore the same pair of pants for two weeks once, a pair of pared down, striped Japanese diplomat's trousers. I reached the point of not wanting to go to school because of those pants.

A hand to mouth existence is what it was and was responsible for my migraine headaches.

Never any quiet. If the people in the basement didn't have a bone to pick, then someone would bring one in.

Fist fights, (my mother and Jean, over the Mother's Day pimp named Red, with whom my mother had lived for awhile) plain ol' thumpin's, (Henry Sr. coming down on Jean's head with his fists), knife slashings, disputes between the junkies about the division of the heroin. Noise.

I was going to Fuller School, getting my first taste of math. It was bitter stuff, almost too much for a head that was busily coping with a lifestyle that caused psychosomatic illnesses. I always tried to stay outside for as long as I could because going home made me sick to the head. And my psyche wasn't getting a much better break out in the street.

There seemed to be nothing I could do to get away from any of it. No money for movies, fantasies, candy, bubble gum, a semi-celibate sex life (I really think I was seeing too many fights between men and women to think romantically).

I felt completely out of pocket. I couldn't fully give my energies over to just hanging out with the fellas. I was hungry, shy, vaguely ashamed of myself. It didn't occur to me that they were going through the same changes.

Those feelings weren't ever total and they were often eliminated by Momma getting money from somewhere. Or by getting a kiss from a pretty girl.

I could dance but I didn't think I could, beyond the two step belly rub. Tracing back, memories. Ashamed of myself isn't exactly the correct expression of what I felt. Maybe ashamed of the circumstances of our life would be closer to the truth.

For example, I had to go to the "relief station" on Cottage Grove once a month to pick up our allotment of potatoes, rubbery cheese, powdered eggs (which rubberized while cooking) and good butter.

I could never seem to find myself enough alleys to duck through, on my way home with those shopping bags of "relief foodstuffs." If only there had been someone near enough to politicize me into understanding that I should've been mad, not ashamed, for being given crumbs from the Big Table.

It was really sad. They had actually convinced the victims that they should be ashamed of being the victims.

Maybe it was just an awkward period but I felt it as deeply as I would ever feel anything.

As usual, I hustled. I returned pop bottles to the store (two cents for the small one, five cents for the large ones), I looked for the means to create a way.

And through the whole business I felt like a stranger to myself. It was as though I were outside of me watching me, watching the sparks fly around inside the left or the right side of my head. The desperate gnawing at the insides from a day on bread and sugared water.

I read too much. The reading seemed to dull my senses, to suspend ugly feelings and at the same time, to sharpen perceptions.

I knew, by the time I was ten, and *definitely* by fourteen, that something was *wrong*. I didn't really know what the connection was between us being Black and poor but I had some inklings.

But it was kind of confusing because the dope peddlers, pimps and star 'hoes were Black and they seemed to have a lot. I couldn't really figure it out.

And then, of course, we were moving on.

We stayed, one night, in a basement behind a coal feeder. The room, you understand, had once been the place where they stored coal, before going "moderne" with the coal feeder.

We had to trip across planks slanted over slimy water and scurrying rats to reach our "apartment." Momma paid a small wad off into an anonymous hand, (damn! anybody ever look at things from a child's perspective?) explained, after the rent business was done, to me and my sister that she had a "run" to make and disappeared for a day and a night.

I couldn't tell what it was that bothered me about the place until she returned and said in the saddest tone I'd ever heard her use, "damn   this place ain't got no windows."

We immediately snatched up our boxes and split.

Memories, the places we lived in.

Some of the changes we went through were so quickly done that it seemed impossible to believe that they had occurred.

Chapter 4

It came to some kind of head at Forrestville Grammar School. I couldn't believe it. In some kind of magical way I was graduating from grammar school. I could not believe it.

My father, an ephemeral, peripheral figure, was there. He gave me an expensive ballpoint pen set. Miss Sweet slipped me a ten spot, which I lost before I left the stage.

Miss Sweet and Mr. Jimmy and Uncle John, alias Sweetmilk, alias Milk, alias "Sonny Boy." People who helped save me. Memories.

I had lived at Miss Sweet and Mr. Jimmy's for a time, before graduating from Forrestville. As a matter of fact they were two of the main reasons for me graduating from grammar school because they gave me a stable point of reference, something the school authorities demanded.

Miss Sweet and Mr. Jimmy, like woven threads through an early fabric in my life. Saviors.

I first knew them, became aware of them on Wentworth Avenue, down the street from White Sox Park. There I was, on a second floor back porch, splashing around in a tub of cool water on a soaking, humid, hot Chicago day.

But even before that they were there; staying with Miss Sweet in a building on 50th and State Street, she did day work and left me with a teenaged girl who had me climb up on top of her and pushed my lil' peepee into a huge, hairy, warm Something. Yeahhh, Miss Sweet and Mr. Jimmy were always there.

The porch came later. It was/is the most beautifully innocent period of life I can recall.

My sister was staying with a lady named Miss Willie; Miss Willie with the terrible welted scar that flashed diagonically across the left side of her face, from temple to chin. Miss Willie, a beautiful woman, all heart and soul.

Miss Sweet (I found out later in life) had had a few nervous breakdowns but never one I could remember. Maybe I was so saturated by people with nervous conditions that I didn't pay it any mind.

She wore a bandanna over her uncombed, permanently kinked hair, an apron with jangling keys and change in the pocket and did "day work" until she was in her seventies.

Mr. Jimmy looked and acted like a Mohawk Indian chief. Being from Detroit, he might've been a chief of something. He definitely looked like an Indian. A gold skinned man with a deep appreciation of the stories that came on the radio, the baseball games and the sweet cravings of a little boy. Man made incredible blackberry pies.

They were the closest things to super-grandparents anyone would ever want to have. When I lived with them I had it made.

They had two sons, Walter and Dike, but they *stayed* in some kind of trouble. Walter became a notorious hype who loved beautiful clothes and finally O.D.'ed while Dike simply riped off everything he felt he could drag or carry.

I guess I was the scapegoat, the one they could all turn to for love. And I did love them very, very much. I loved Miss Sweet because she was both practical and sweet and Mr. Jimmy, because he indulged me.

It was like being in a kind of enchanted place with them. Big front room with San Francisco high ceilings, middle-dining room, huge kitchen and a room off to the back where coal was stored for winter.

Enough room, more than enough room. Food to eat, real food. Pork chops, rice, cream styled corn, rye bread, butter, milk, red soda pop, real food.

Mr. Jimmy got home from working at the Eagle laundry, had his dinner off a tray and afterwards we listened to the radio—Fibber McGee and Molly, Sherlock Holmes, the Shadow, Bob Hope, whoever.

I have to think that a whole group of unknown radio writers had a lot to do with my education. I listened and imaged. What else could you do with a radio?

I loved listening to the radio with Mr. Jimmy. He smoked pipes and cigars, had a beautifully developed paunch, snow drift hair, this Indian profile and could say the nastiest things in the most gentle way. Rabelasian shit.

I played with caterpillars and rerouted ants over pieces of peppermint stick in front of their house. They drank red soda pop (Mr. Jimmy, sometimes beer) with dinner and I was the one designated to take the empty bottles back and pick up a fresh bottle.

My duties were extremely light, my migraines never happened when I was with them and there was no one to fight. No one in the neighborhood fought; we fought the white boys in the next neighborhood.

Weird battleground. We/they had picked an area way/alley

that led from the predominantly Black neighborhood to the predominantly white neighborhood as the place to throw bottles at each other. It was a weird scene.

We'd be leaping around like monkeys at one end of the alley and they'd be leaping around like monkeys at the other end. Strangely I don't remember anyone being hit or cut from the bottles flying back and forth.

It was a truly stupid way to behave. We didn't call each other names or anything, we just threw bottles and ducked and dodged. It would be difficult to say why we were doing it.

Mr. Jimmy baked blackberry pies for me. They were sweet enough to draw bees but I didn't give a damn about cavities and I loved them. They called me "Pa" (because I seemed so wise) and treated me the way they felt a little boy should be treated.

I was always happy with them. Memories

A lil' breeze tonight and it carries me to a cold day on a corner in Chicago. I was appointed a lieutenant of patrol boys at Forrestville Grammar School, freezing my ass off because my teacher thought I was "a nice boy."

On the strength of the same breeze; living on Oakenwald Avenue, across the railroad tracks from Lake Michigan, 47th and Oakenwald. Me, sleeping in the kitchen of a two room "apartment" that never seemed to receive any heat, made you feel a real kinship with Siberia. Years later.

I slept in the kitchen on an Army cot, under a grim brownish Army blanket that had one of the weirdest holes in it I had ever been exposed to. Really weird hole; it managed, somehow, to always leave a vital part of my anatomy uncovered, no matter which way I turned.

I slept with my head practically buried in the oven but the breezes whistling through the kitchen cut the heat off from every part of my body but the top of my head.

The kitchen window faced the lake and on a clear summer

day it offered a spectacularly lovely view of the lake. It was like we were sharing what the Gold Coasters took for granted, from the second floor of the ghetto.

The winter scene was something else. I cannot name the winter that drove me into my first wife's malevolent embrace but I do recall thinking   shit! anything would be better than this.

Norma, memories, scars . . .

Sitting up here this evening (two days before Halloween) buzzed on an excellent cognac after a beautiful day it seems appropriate that I should be on Norma, the Normaian section of things, for pure contrast.

I had no preparation for a Norma. My life, up to her bombardment of my existence had been relatively simple; Black, slums, Soweto, U.S.A.

If anyone would've asked me what I was doing at Wilson Junior College in 1956, I wouldn't've known what to tell them. I had no idea of "becoming" one thing or the other. Nor did I care about the whole thing.

Sister Moffett was responsible for me being there but I couldn't attach a purpose to my presence on the junior collegiate scene. The things that I had thought about getting involved with were not listed in the college catalogue.

Maybe Regina Sweirzinski and her dog Tinka would be a good place to find Norma's origins.

Memories. 1957. Racial relations, per usual, between us and *them*, were not at good level.

I'd never really had anything to do with white women. Black women, sisters, had been my sole/soul psycho/sexual experience up to this time and they had done such an effervescently good job on my psyche that I had not even imagined that there were other people worth doing it to/with.

Talking about something deep here. The "racial" ladies, my sister-women who had offered themselves and their

43

experience were phenomenons, everyone. No chauvinism here, just the soul truth.

They offered it, despite the terrible consequences of a life with three or four babies wagging behind them 'cause you could be certain that it would happen. The sisters may not have been offering heap big bucks or a mansion in the Heavens (the white boy had already put a corrupt bankruptcy note on her existence).

Norma's appearance in my life was a freak occurrence. Regina Sweirzinski, the blind Polish princess and her loyal dog, Tinka, I could understand. She was outside the laws of American raciality. Blind since twenty (twenty-three now, then) real blonde, sincerely Polish, haughty, stacked, out there, blind.

I guess I got fucked around by her blindness. Up until her happening in on the scene I had never related to a blind person, of any racial persuasion.

She was purely pre-Norma. It happened in Mr. Morris Tisch's English lit class. Morris Tisch, that cold blooded little Polish Jew with the craft to teach.

I sat next to her, watching her Braille her way through class for a few months. I could've been a moth too near the flame or a black snake flicking his tongue out at the atmosphere. In any case, we started talking.

Sometimes, after class, we'd sit next to each other and say nothing. She'd stare at the blackboard as though she were reading the prof's original notes and I'd stare at Tinka, the wonder dog, who'd glare at me. Never had had anything to do with a dog who glared back at me.

Sometimes, after class, we'd talk. I don't remember what we talked about but it was seductive, on both sides. There wasn't much else that Tinka would allow us to get away with before she started barking. Or worse yet, barking in a baritone growl.

Real Bohemian stuff we were, for the times. One evening

44

we stayed after school to see the Wilson Junior College Drama Theatre in *A Streetcar Named Desire*. And Tinka prevented me from doing anything more than feeling Regina's luscious right hand with real serious growling and one coldblooded bark.

Blind, blonde, stacked and Polish. Never could get around to dealing with my real feelings. But it was all definitely Pre-Norma. It had to be because she would never have allowed a rival to survive.

Norma, a whole horde of warped identities.

I spotted her sweater first, bumping and grinding through the passageway between Wilson Junior College and Chicago Teachers College, the connection between the two years of A.A. and the four years of B.A.

After a few months of casually observing brothers shoot at white girls, I had discovered one basic truth—white girls were not into nuances in 1957, they were into brothers. And vice versa.

Hard to say where Norma was, philosophically. White woman, rejecting conservative River Grove, Illinois norms. Or whatever. Different kinda woman.

It's always difficult to connect certain types of people to certain eras, movements, moments. Norma definitely settled into that category.

Scene: It is the middle of the afternoon on a super Spring day in Chicago, the kind of day in Chicago, on the lakefront, that causes middle management types to roll their pants legs up past their calves and gaze at the sky.

Norma and I, taking advantage of the feeling, must have had one of the briefest, most blatant fucks ever seen by hundreds of lunch time office workers in Chicago, underneath a Grant Park hedge.

Dumb me, lost in this woman's thighs, had no idea that they were there.

Like I said, I spotted her sweater first. Memories.

No cool on my part in the school passageway.

"Hey look, I dig you, gimme your phone number 'n stuff" etc., etc., etc.

She, months later, having discovered how po' I was: "why don't you come to my house for dinner on Thursday?"

She didn't tell me that her parents were to the right of Hitler when it came to racial relations. Like, really bad.

Fuck it! I says to myself. I don't care about anything. All I can understand is that I've managed to catch this major league specimen of a white woman.

Norma was a large boned, full bodied representative of the Teutonic ideal. Fear makes joy.

I fucked my way into Norma (after a few others, I might add). It was an undesirable way to approach her but, like I said, I didn't care about anything.

There was a saying at the time: "If you scratch a white bitch seriously enough, you'll come across some money." Being poor meant that I was already serious, from git. Any rationale would do.

Awright, here we go. One snowed out winter evening we got on a surburban train and rode and rode and rode and then transferred, finally stumbling off in River Grove, Illinois. I had no idea where I was until I discovered that all of the disembarking passengers were white. No matter where we were that simple fact spelled trouble.

Strangely, no one created a problem, beyond fierce stares and folks mumbling weirdly. In Chicago's suburbs, please remember, around about this time, African-Americans were slaughtered regularly.

Her mother peeked at me through at a two inch door opening and almost fainted. I can still see her eyes wall back to the whites. We were obviously in for a fantastic evening.

Brilliant woman, this Norma, brilliant but warped. I can

say that evenly, nourished by all of the objectivity that the years have given me.

We had this enormous physical thing going on, which put a bunch of other colder feelings on hold for awhile. We were not actually madly in love, we were simply mad.

In a kindergarten mercenary way I saw her as a means to escape my cot in the kitchen. She wasn't beautiful but she was stacked and she was wide open. It took me a bit to discover how wide open she really was.

Dinner in her home; River Grove, Illinois. Lots of snow outside, no place to hide. The meal was solid, European, bland. Meat, potatoes, stuff to stick to your ribs. I longed for a pepper or a bottle of tabasco, something that would make me feel warm about what was happening.

Her father, Charles, put in an appearance after his before dinner nap, took one startled look at me and disappeared, never to be seen again that evening. I found him to be a pro at that over the succeeding years.

Really interesting din-din. Mother, Norma, her son Stephen (surprise!) and I. She had slipped in and out of a teenaged marriage at sixteen or so and had a son to show for it.

Beautiful example of a little white boy. Blonde, blue eyed, pale skinned, spoiled. I don't recal what the dessert was or how the dinner came to an end, but it did and I was returned to the world of extreme poverty. None of it seemed real.

We proceeded to screw around for the course of one hot winter. We screwed in her fat friend's basement apartment on Lake Shore Drive (I had passed the place a thousand times during my delivery boy days at Carnegie Drugstore). We screwed in parked cars in front of friends' homes.

I remember hearing the question, "why don't they come inside?" We screwed in the school library, in the record booth, listening to the 1812 Overture. Anywhere the urge provoked us.

Her challenge to me was "are you as bold as I am?" and,

47

like a madman, I took the challenge. I was mad because the climate of the times made me a semi-legal target for snipers, weirdos, racists, any nut who disliked the sight of a Black man with a white woman. I was lucky.

Memories . . .

The spring of 1957; sprawled out on the lakefront at the end of 43rd Street, the raggedy back porch of the ol' homestead visible across the train tracks, sucking on each others tongues.

She: "Why don't we get our own place?"

He: "That would really be a good idea."

It was a classic case of manipulation. She had one thing in her mind and I had something completely different on my mind.

After an hour more of tongue sucking, we strolled back across the bridge to my "home," (my mother already knew Norma, we had been caught in bed that winter) slid up to where Momma was snapping string beans. (Poor people used to eat lots of health foods—greens, beans, molasses, stuff like that.)

I was stunned to the last nerve when I heard Norma tell my mother that we wanted to get married. Married?! Nineteen years old, with my whole life in front of me! The last thing I could imagine was being married. Living together, sharing expenses, roommates maybe, but married?!

We got married. A stiff ass Lutheran service performed by a big ol' German named Shuller. Or was it Schultz?

Memories   must flashback here for a moment.

Chapter 5

It is the day/night before our marriage and we are staying in the ultra bohemian apartment (1957 variety) of Beverly and Howard. And her brother and another guy and maybe another person. Or whoever. That kind of pad.

The beds were mattresses on salvaged doors, pre-Hippie. Norma, at one point during the night, leaves our pre-nuptial bed to trip down the hallway to the john. After an uncomfortably long time, new-bride-groom-to-be-that-I-am, I decide to see what the hell as happened to my bride-to-be. Is she constipated? What?

I tippy toe through the hall leading to the shitter. On my way I pass this door from whence comes the sound of people doin' it. Lo 'n behold!, my sizzling ears tell me, it is my bride-to-be and Beverly's brother! Hmmmmmmmm.

I tippy toe-stumble back to our mattress on the door, stretch myself out and think, real hard. Hmmmmmmmm. Right then 'n there I had this deep in the gut feeling that we weren't going to live happily ever after.

Meanwhile, the dance started.

Memories, scars, absurd shit. Racial prejudice within an interracial marriage. The first time she screamed, "Nigger!" I felt as though my skin had been sliced off of my body.

We fought, physically, all over. On one occasion, we fought on an "El" train—from Chicago and State Street to 63rd and Kimbark. Strong lady. It took as many left hooks and right crosses as I could uncork to keep her honest. Strong lady. Despite my carefully planted hooks and jabs, there were times when her buzz saw tactics would penetrate my defense and I'd wind up with a face full of scratches.

Wars of nerves. Can I stay awake another night arguing with this woman? What the hell have we been arguing the last three nights about anyway? "Uhhh, baby, what're you doin', standing over me like that? With that golf club over your shoulder?"

Nerves. "Norma!, what the hell are you doing?!"

"I don't want to live, leave me alone!"

"Quick! operator! please send me an ambulance to 1727 East 71st Street, my wife has cut her wrists!"

Three suicide attempts? Four suicide attempts? By the time the last one happened, I was casually hoping she'd succeed.

Really different feeling to come home three times in a month and find your wife sitting in the bathtub, buck fuckin' nekkid, bleeding from wrist slashes.

Promiscuity. We both did a lot of that. The emotional temper of the times, pre-1960's, was absolutely perfect for those avant-garde enough to have read or heard enough or felt enough to want to be sexually uninhibited. After all, the worse that could happen would be a hard case of clap. Someone must have had herpes back then but no one ever heard of it.

Memories . . . Mexico City. We left our year old daughter with a couple of Norma's friends, (a Black couple, believe it or not) her son Stephen with her parents in River Grove and off we go.

I have no idea why we decided on Mexico City rather than some other place, but I'm sure that certain sections of Mexico City still wish that we had tripped to some other sector of the world.

We fought up and down the Paseo de la Reforma at midnight. And midday. We got sloppy drunk and disgraced ourselves in any number of places, at different times.

Example: It's late, 'round about twoish. The lady must have a snack before we return to the Maria Cristina Hotel.

"I must have a snack before we return to the Maria Cristina."

I suggest a taco.

"Who the hell wants a taco?"

Fifty taco stands within ten paces of us bristled up and threatened to close in on us.

"Well, what the hell do you want then?"

"I said   I want a snack!"

My impulse was to leave the crazy bitch out in the streets and go on back to the hotel room but I just couldn't. I don't know what Mexico City is like now, but at the time a single woman (a white woman at that) on the streets after dark could get her ass snatched off.

A snack. We wound up in a posh restaurant that was ninety-nine percent closed. She persuaded the owner, the waiters, the mariachis, the dishwashers, everyone on the premises, that they should serve one more meal to/for this romantic couple from Los Estados Unidos.

Duck Ala Orange, etc., etc. They put the pot on for us. And the mariachis crooned and yelped and the waiters pranced and beamed. The dishwashers peeked out through the swinging doors. They, in a word, styled us.

The meal was finally over, the singing done, the smiling

51

over, pay up time.

I had just enough to pay the bill (a snack, shit!), with four centavos left over.

"Uh, Norma, can you leave a tip? I'm cleaned out of pesos."

"Tip? What tip?"

After the beer, wine and cognac I should've been somewhat tipsy. I wasn't. Trouble ahead cleared my brain in a second.

"We have to tip these people, honey," I whispered, trying to impress her with the serious tone of my voice.

"Fuck 'em!" she announced, picking duck meat out of her teeth.

It didn't take a bunch of English for several of the people bunched around our table to pick up the drift of matters. Suddenly I saw the Hyde and Jekyll of the Mexican surface. From the smiling, crooning, beaming, warm faces a change, not that I blamed them.

The owner rescued us from a Mexican lynch mob. He eased us back out into the night; I hate to think what they would've done to us if he hadn't. None of it made a rat's ass to the baby, and she had had her snack.

Something was always happening. She had a two day affair with a slick Peruvian down the hall from us. I tried to cop his wife in retaliation and failed.

We created a new level of life for the tradition oriented Mexicans to deal with. The trip was both horrendous and wonderful. Norma was horrendous but Mexico City was wonderful. I'd never been outside the country and Mexico was happening!

The murals on the University walls blew my mind. And the Mexican people. I made a discovery that has lasted until this day.

Wandering through the park near our hotel we struck up a conversation with a white dude, a doctor from San Francisco, and his beautiful brown Mexican lady. Friendly dude, away from the rat race in the States, he invited us to lunch.

It wasn't until we were watching the second bull of the afternoon in the Plaza Mexico that it dawned on me that I had shared a lovely lunch, enjoyed the warmth of a stranger's home and experienced no bad vibes. The only negative thing about the whole experience is that I was on the scene with a person who hated Mexicans ("they're filthy!"), was prejudiced toward Blacks and had a pale consideration for most other people. She wasn't a Bundist or anything overtly Hitlerian. Her dislike was equivalent to a very strong quirk, like, if I don't like myself, why should I like anybody else? Lady was fucked up in the psyche.

We splurged down to nickels and dimes in Mexico City and had to take separate buses back to Chicago. She wanted us, of course, to ride the same bus. I killed, vetoed, nayed and fled from the idea.

My mind's eye photographed a picture of the two of us fighting, somewhere in the middle of Texas; I'm snatched off the bus and lynched at the side of the road by a mob as she chuckles along.

Texas in 1958 was bad enough without her, I can imagine what it would've been with her. Scene—three people going through customs at the Texas-Mexican border, hot day. Real hot. I have a bottle of rum in my bag, cheap, from Mexico. Redneck Customs Officer: "What's this?"

He drops the bottle on the concrete, it breaks. He checks my identification. I have a picture of my wife in the glassine section.

Redneck Customs Officer: "Who is this?"

Me: (Hesitantly) "A   my   uh, friend's wife."

Redneck Customs Officer: "That what y'all do up Nawth, run 'round wid each others wives pictures in each others wallets? He, yo' friend, gotta picture o' yo' wife in his wallet?"

I was tempted to laugh. Dear Norma, the bitch could even cause me problems in absentia. A Jimmy Stewart type was summoned to take me to an office where I was forced to undress for a search.

The search uncovered nothing but my body. I was allowed to exit before being called back for another strip. And another. And another. It went on for about six and a half times. It was a helluva price to pay for having a white woman's flick in my wallet.

By the time the trip through Texas was done I had made a decision. We had to split, no ifs, buts, or ands about it. We had to split.

My friends all asked the same question. Why did it take so long? My answer varied with the intensity of the questioner. Usually, to be honest, I'd simply say, "I wanted to make it work."

Ironically, another white woman came to my financial rescue, in order to file the paper s and have the business done that would legally grant me freedom. My sanity would never be the same.

The other white woman was an unusual figure in the world. Small, garrulous creature with a semi-Churchillian shape, lovely intelligence and a strong urge for Ten High whiskey and playing cards.

Eve in the Gardens she was; Altgeld Gardens was a ninety-nine percent Black project system somewhere to the south of downtown Chicago. A friend of mine introduced us and my mercenary nature fed me the adrenalin to do the rest.

"Eve, can you loan me three hundred dollars to pay my attorney's fees?"

Eve, from Leicester, England, warm, beautiful person with four loving children who used to sometimes mimic her heavy mid-English brogue.

"Three hundred dollars, you shay? Is thot all?"

Chapter 6

The nightmare was over. I took the girlchild we had made over to my mother's room in the Almo Hotel (she had moved back again) and got about the study of becoming a bachelor. I thought the divorce would spell out the complete end for us, but then, I've always been the optimistic type.

Moving to a room in the building called the Avon (61st and Dorchester) I attempted to jerk myself free of the emotional chain that had been wound around my psychological throat. I stepped off into the pit and went wild for a taste. Norma stepped up her activities too.

She had somehow or other discovered lesbianism, which meant that on many occasions she and her "man" would be knocking on my door at two a.m., full of beer and malevolence.

Let me put *old* Norma on hold for a bit, and offer a nugget from a later period. Years after our number had been played, on a visit to Chicago, I spotted her on 47th Stret, near Calumet.

There she was, grinding, twisting and bumping her way back to her office (a social worker) munching a box of popcorn. I had no time to hide. She spotted me. We greeted each other civilly, chatted on the busy street for a bit. The "new" Norma.

She suggested that we have a drink for "old times sake."

Grand Hotel, 51st and South Parkway (King Drive now). A drink. Two drinks, three drinks. Maybe four. Enough to unlock undercurrent thoughts

We're in a hotel bar, why don't we rent a room and knock off a lil' piece, "for old times sake?"

The rotten bitch must have had one of the most virulent forms of the claps packed inside her cunt that I'd ever been exposed to. Within two days my penis was dripping green pus like Niagara Falls.

As the crusty old moralist of a doctor plunged his needle into my left buttock cheek I had to smile . . . same ol' Norma, full of the expected.

Weird spirit of an era, that sector I sometimes think of as the Hyde Park-Avon Towers Era. 1959-'62, right about through there. Most of the months during '59-'60 flicker through my mind as a blur.

Scene: Dark brown skinned lady with darker circles under her eyes offers me a couple wake up pills because I am nodding on my post office seat, zipped out from a late night and an earlier day—wine, women and zip.

I say, "thanks" for the pills, pop the bad little pink boys and instantly awake. Incredible sensation. Quick!!

Two weeks later, having experienced enough of the sensation to begin to love it, I copped a jar of a thousand. One thousand Dexedrine tablets   I was off 'n running!

Marvelous little sectino of life in the ultra fast lane, absolutely on a hummer. Having grown up ground a mainly smoking-drinking-gambling-group of people I wasn't prepared for pill poppin'.

I understood heroin, of course, from my years with the dope fiends, but this was something else, this was The Dexie!

I'm amazed that I didn't kill myself with those fucking pills. Funny   I flash on my body ripping 'n running through the streets, going somewhere or nowhere. Doesn't/didn't matter, the pills were in charge.

I must've been in the best shape of my life. I ran, I didn't jog. I ran in and out of people's homes, their lives, everyone was falling in love with me and I was falling in love back. It must've had something to do with the elusive nature of my lifestyle at that time.

I don't really know what it was exactly, the times, my attitude, the place I was living in. What?! Maybe it had something to do with being free of Norma. Or maybe it was the place.

The place was called the Avon, on 61st and Dorchester, southeast corner. An incredible place in 1959 or any other time. Ninety-five percent male, (during the course of the normal work week) lots of Africans, wild West Indians, a smattering of Panamanians, an Irishman or two, bunch of avant garde Afro-American originals, a heap of world students.

Four floors of ideas, bizarre reasons, bristling intelligence (like, there were no dummies in the Avon, none) brutally heterosexual.

We used to have All-Building parties, from time to time. Check this out: Someone, probably one of the West Indians (Donovan or Brown), threw out the idea and by Saturday morning it was in fullest bloom.

Four floors and a basement, something like twelve rooms on each floor, each filled with a party loving monster. An All-Building Party.

The word was flashed all the way to the northside. "They're having a great party at the Avon!"

We wandered into and out of each others rooms, feasting, drinking and fucking for two days. In some circles one is still apt to hear the boast, "I survived the first All-Building Party at the Avon."

The place was filled, even when there were no parties, with as much drama, comedy, tragedy, love, or whatever made human beings sensitive as a person could possibly deal with.

Love, yes, love had a lot to do with the atmosphere. We were living as brothers, peacefully.

It wasn't the faddish liberalism of Hyde Park, none of that. This was the real thing.

We were real to the point of loaning each other money. And, from time to time, exchanging ladies.

"Uhh, dig, man, could I get a piece of that. I mean, would you mind?"

"If she don't care, I don't care. It ain't my ass."

"What should I   how should I go about it?"

"Ask her if you could have some pussy? Simple."

1959, lots of people were just being liberated. For the first time in my life I had a decent income, a place to live in that suited my fantasies.

The women. So many women. I can close my eyes and see faces, personalities, breasts, the left one belonging to one woman, the right to another.

They were mostly Black and white women, but in between an American Indian might step through. Or a Kurd. Or a Hindu. Or a Tibetan. Or someone who was a combination of all of the aforementioned.

Working at the post office gave me social access to hundreds of working women, who felt quite independent, earning their own money and were quite likely to do whatever they liked.

The Black women came straight from the job, the white women came from Hyde Park and the Northside, everybody else came from wherever.

The flavors, the mixtures were enchanting. The morning with a Jewish princess whose father-friend-slave fried her eggs to order. The afternoon with an African-American Earth-sister who could put so much love on you that it would cause the Earth to bounce, not simply move.

Brilliant women, sexy women, crazy, kind, funny, absurd. Helena, the Greek whore who thought she was Melina Mercouri was absurd. We were no better. The greedy sexists who winked to each other when we closed our doors for the day or evening's activities.

In any case, the joy of it all is what sticks out, no pun intended. The feeling one could have, strolling through the halls, knowing that there was a ninety percent chance (especially on Saturday nights) that most of the people on that floor, in the building, were making love. I suspect that we sometimes fell under the spirit of a kind of erotic group pressure. The halls glowed with it.

I'm sure that there must've been homosexuals in the place, but the heterosexual element was brutally overwhelming.

I don't remember doing much writing, other than "juicy" letters. I wouldn't've been able to say that I was a writer during this period, the way some dudes were claiming to be photographers. Or musicians.

However, it was a very fermentive time for me. Aside from the sensual, there was a tremendously stimulating intellectualism in the Avon. You could step into anybody's room and get an education of one kind or another.

Memories

Moist night, juicy raindrops, a Chicago summer evening rain. Judy and I are on the roof of the building, being sprinkled on by the mist whipping past the forest of wires.

Judy is small, fine boned, a New Orleans high yaller lady, and so really charming, intelligent and feminine that I have trouble believing that she is real. I have persuaded her to be naked with me on the roof; she, coming from a "normal" background, is freaked out by the feeling of the moment.

We wind up sprawling on the roof, curled up in a sexual knot, oblivious to the tar, gravel and wires. The sky roared when we climaxed.

Memories

The Hyde Park Party was happening. The Hyde Park Party

somebody intrusively strumming his guitar over there, determined that he is going to get the crowd to join him for a folky song-singalong. God! how did Pete Seeger do it?

"Avant garde" multi-racial group, mostly white, a quartet of Blacks who wear black horn rims, (male and female) talk intelligent-animatedly, are properly costumed and know how to behave in a way that doesn't distress white Liberals.

The two Black women are the sweetheart and wife of two white dudes, respectively. The two Black men are divided. One thinks he's white and the other one wishes he were. People secretly piss them off by relating to them as though they were the only Blacks at the party.

And, from time to time, other types arrived. A brother, for example, who is simply swaying from side to side, loaded on some mella 'erb, looking for a white girl to have a good time on.

And his pink nippled counterpart, eyes glazed, lips wetted and parted, having made two recent decisions, after she came to grips with where her head was at, really.

Number one, she was not going to be the frustrated creature her mother was and, number two, she was determined to find out if Black dudes had bigger ding dongs.

Lots of wine drinking, some surreptitious reefer smoking, (it was at that point where a lot of ladies didn't get high publicly, no matter how hip they were supposed to be) a little belly rubbing as the evening warmed up.

Some silly ass behavior, usually by some white girl who had decided to throw an attention-spasm-tantrum for one reason or another. Maudlin tears, drunken slurs, "fuck everything!", gross behavior, the types who used to announce that they were "trying to get their heads together." They were also likely to say "like" at odd spaces in conversations. "Like."

I thought too much of the Hyde Park scene was sheer bullshit, for a simple number of reasons.

The greatest one was that it took too much, psychologically, out of the Black people. The Hyde Park Party was supposed to be where you came to pretend that racism was the exotic title of a Swedish author's book.

At that point I must've heard some white person say, at least fifty times, "I don't pay any attention to a person's color, people are just people to me."

There were a half dozen variations on that theme. We all circled each other, drinking our wine, darting into the heap from time to time, to pull out a pink pussy, a girl friend with coins, a liberal, sometimes a wife.

I was going ass backwards. I had already gone through the interracial marriage scene just as everybody else seemed to be revving up to go for it.

The conversations were straight out of a fishbowl, carefully sculptured and designed to appear dangerous, but not really listened to.

Jimmy's tavern on 55th and Woodlawn was a hotbed of the shit, beer by the pitcher, chess at the tables against the wall, intellectualism running rampant, "mixed couples," integration, so much sham and pretense.

The casually understood agreement we all immediately made across the fence was that we would not disclose the fact that the white boy was *not* hip. The situation led to a bunch of badly concealed disillusionments.

Swinging slightly away from the Hyde Park Party, onto other facets. Usually, after enough psychohistroy had been exchanged, something could/would happen.

Jewish girls from unorthodox backgrounds would do lots of unkosher stuff. Wasp type guys would get reddish in the face and start proclaiming their admiration for Marcus Garvey and Malcom X. (Some of them might get a lil' crazed on the subject after a couple hits on a reefer. Reefer madness?)

Of course, here and there there were still isolated instances of simply groovy people being fo' real.

I saw us, the Blacks, giving a rich feeling to the scene but at the same time we were supposed to be just like everybody else.

Shit! the white boys couldn't even dance (this was pre-Soul Train). If we hadn't been on the scene the Hyde Park Party would have been a great gray dud.

I checked out how hard it was for the brothers 'n sisters, how utterly hip or how utterly square they/we had to be, just to hang ourselves around the white people. They didn't, on the other hand, seem to be giving anything up.

In most instances they had not been through very much, were not as honest with themselves or the people they pretended to relate to, nor were they particularly interesting, once we got past the color section.

Comin' from where I was comin' from, a lot of the bullshit that they were supposed to be hung up on didn't make a lot of sense to me. I mean, like, what kind of cohesion were you supposed to have with some people who were telling you that they were dropping out of something you had never been privileged to be in?

It was interesting though, while it lasted. Periodically I find myself at some variation of the Hyde Park Party and I always, but always, try to ease away from the scene as soon as possible.

It was a rich period, in many ways. People seemed more romantic or was there simply less smog in the air?

I drifted. I went to take my daughter out on the weekends, to a movie and a milk shake. She was so cute and said so many profoundly funny things.

She was living with my mother in the old Almo Hotel, surrounded by the same people I was raised with (they never left the building or changed). They weren't people you would deliberately choose to be around unless you were one of them. If you weren't one of them and you lived around them, you'd have to at least make an effort to understand them. That's what I think an education should be.

Chapter 7

Anyway, the hedonistic train clattered on. I went everywhere and did everything. Some of it was purely stupid. Two immediate examples come to mind.

I was riding the bus one night, coming home from somewhere. Very interesting blonde woman with high Slavic cheekbones and glazed blue eyes flirts with me in the ninety-nine percent empty bus.

Norma temporarily out of my psyche, I flirt back. The flirtatious glances become full fledged hot looks. We are attracted to each other. Serendipity on the move, for certain.

We get off the bus at the same stop, she has a charming, wistful, almost sad way of smiling. I like her smile and her shape, we wind up in a real sleazy hotel on 63rd Street.

I felt it strange to find a virgin willing to go directly from a public bus to a private, scumbag hotel. And she had to be a virgin, the most virginal virgin I'd ever met.

In the B-movie flickering neon light periodically bathing our scene I could see the wistful-sad smile. I could also see the beautiful body. The form, nude, was a catatonic ice cube. I started getting really scared about four thirty in the morning, when I realized that her glazed blue eyes were still glazed and her smile was still where it had been in the beginning.

Her virginity was still intact too . . . not because we hadn't made a couple stabs at it but because my penis had been stunned into submission by the cement-hardness of her vaginal lips.

Curiously, investigating the matter closely under the bedside lamp, I stare at what seems to be a normal looking pussy. The only thing is that the whole area is hard, like an old pink tire.

We re-dressed at dawn and tripped back out into the streets. I was more than puzzled. She seemed to like to be with me but her expression never changed. Feeling the need for some counseling I steered her over to Margie and David's pad. David, the eccentric sociologist, Margie, David's eccentric wife.

"Odie," Margie whispers to me after surreptitiously going through the lady's purse, "this woman has either run away from Manteno or she's on some kind of leave. In any case, she isn't one of society's regulars."

I'm sure I blinked in surprise. Manteno was the asylum for hurt minds. She was a hurt mind. I almost got the shakes thinking about the night I had just spent with her.

We gently took her downtown and put her back on the train to Manteno. She was still smiling her wistful sexy-sad little smile as the train pulled out. I thanked my friends for their diagnostic aid and slunk away to a troubled afternoon of attempted sleep.

Several nights later, walking west on 61st Street, loaded, feeling unusual about something, I spot this short lady with a scarf on her head strolling in front of me. It wasn't exactly lust that took me to her side, I like to think it was a brand of gallantry.

"Uhhh, 'cuse me, are you awright? I mean, it's pretty dangerous to be walking around out here this late."

"Well, why don't you take me home then?"

"Where do you live?"

"I'm talkin' about your home, fool."

Dark woman, liquid laugh, velvet sense of humor, out looking for something. I understood.

We linked arms and headed back toward the Avon. I never saw her face. I wouldn't recognize it if I looked straight at her but I'll never forget her breasts.

In my room, dim light on, the seductionists' glow worm, she undressed. I had my back turned for a minute, thinking of how lucky I was to have found somebody to fuck through the midnight hours with.

She was a short, brown-skinned sister with breasts that fell down to her thighs. Talk about pendulous. I couldn't believe it.

I must've stared at her breasts for five minutes. In some weird way she managed to keep her face in the shadows, but this beautifully modulated voice oozed out at me.

"I know, they are kinda big, huh?"

I didn't know what to say. I didn't want to make love with her, I didn't want to have anything to do with her, I didn't want to have the feeling of having suckled on the end of an inner tube, 'cause I knew this was going to be something I had to do.

We made ferocious love, despite my inner protests, I fumbled off the edge of the bed for one of her titties, kissed the nipple and fell into a mammarized slumber.

The next morning she was gone. Never will be able to forget those breasts. That kind of thing was always happening to me in Chicago, meeting strange people.

Two homosexual encounters happened that way. One, as a fourteen year old, strolling on Prairie, near 48th Street, the day before Mother's Day.

"Hey, you wanna make five dollars?"

"Doin' what?" I wasn't stupid, I knew you couldn't get something for nothing, even then.

"You don't have to do anything, I'll do all the work."

"Five dollars?"

"Yeah, five dollars."

"O.K."

We went to his apartment a half block away. He showed me pictures of himself as a professional singer and then opened my trousers and sucked my penis for a few minutes.

I observed the whole business as though from a distance, surprised to see myself aroused and in this man's mouth. Everything seemed ridiculous but the five dollar bill in my fist.

He didn't turn me on. I couldn't get any real satisfaction out of what he did and after it was over, I bought my mother a Mother's Day gift with the five spot and forgot about the whole episode.

Years later, in Jimmy's, a very blonde guy followed me outside and asked me if I would "stick my dick in his ass?"

I asked for ten dollars. My price had escalated, inflation. He agreed to the price and we went to his place. After having guzzled a half gallon of beer that evening, I think I could've stuck my dick into anybody's ass.

He hardened me up with a few juicy sucks, slapped some vaseline in his crack and sprawled on his belly.

I studied the whole setup for a few seconds, closed my eyes and plunged in. Clinically, I pumped away for a minute or so and got up. It was no good for me. I may just as well have had my prick in a jar of macaroni or a bowl of cold oatmeal. I couldn't come and that's what I wanted to do. I felt trapped.

I felt very wise after that encounter, knowing what homosexuals did with each other, something to catalogue in my head. It was always that way with me, I'd try anything once. Anything. I guess I was loading up for a writing lifetime and didn't realize it.

Every day, every night, for years, something like that was going on. Working at the post office helped a lot, experiencing that kind of boredom was the catalyst for a whole bunch of stuff.

Modessa and Rosa   memories

"Say man, you wanna come to an orgy?"

"Yeah, why not?"

Brother B., a mahogany cross between Abraham Lincoln and the latest Gregory Peck, his main lady out of town for the moment, (she was actually getting an abortion) had decided to do something off brand. An orgy? Yeah, why not?

The cast of hundreds that was supposed to have been there didn't appear, but we did wind up with some bodies.

Brother B., who had only recently turned his tweed three piece in for sandals and gauzey nightshirts, Gino, a track man whose name I can't recall along with myself, all blatant heterosexuals. Two women put in an appearance, Modessa and Rosa.

Rosa, aahhhhh, Rosa. Rosa I knew from the post office. Every day that she punched in and tripped to wherever she was scheduled to work she slowed production down at least sixty percent for a few minutes. Some of the foremen used to grind their teeth together and pull their hair out when she passed their section.

It was her titties and her personality that did it. First, her titties. Lady was a small, beautifully formed, dark skinned sister with extremely well shaped breasts. They were larger than average but not udderly large. And she carried herself well.

One of those women who offered the world a gorgeous front and was proud of it. I loved her. Everybody loved her.

Modessa. From the moment I saw her the label Tigress came to my head.

Large boned, fluid moving sister, light snuff brown, smooth. It would've taken a Black Reubens to describe her on canvas. About one hundred seventy five pounds, not an ounce of fat anywhere and game as she could be.

I smiled to myself as we settled in with drinks and the Chicago light green. An orgy with these two? I didn't see the dimmest possibility of it happening. They might fuck us to smithereens but we weren't very likely to have an authentic orgy.

After enough wine and smoke, Brother B. herds Gino and myself into the kitchen for a sex conference, the trackman had split for some reason, maybe he'd sensed that the distance would be too much for him.

Brother B., all fired up on gin 'n weed, suggests that we three get buck naked, stroll back into the other room and get it on!

Gino, a herd type, agrees and undresses. I hold back. My argument is that these two ladies have obviously seen it all and done it all and they were not likely to be arbitrarily aroused by the sight of three naked male bodies.

B. and G. disagree. As free spirits in a democratic atmosphere, we decided to go for the individual path.

Brother B. strolls back in with nothing on but an elks tooth around his neck. Gino follows with a slight paunch and a retarded erection. I make another gin 'n tonic and pull off my shirt. What the hell, it's a hot night. I can get that far into it.

Modess and Rosa didn't seem to notice anything different about our appearances. It was semi-funny.

Brother G., exasperated, finally bent over Rosa's chair and asked, "What do you see?"

She looked up and down his lean frame and answered, dead pan, "Some kinda funny lookin' tooth."

Fortunately everybody had a sense of humor and, after a few feeble attempts to persuade the ladies to get nude (they politely nodded no, no) B. and Gino got dressed and decided to enjoy themselves without an orgy.

Meanwhile I had studied the situation carefully and decided to make my move on Rosa.

"Lady digs you," she whispered in my ear as we belly rubbed. Lady is what Rosa called Modessa. Lady digs me?

I didn't quite know how to deal with that. One thing was obvious to me by this time. I wanted some sexual intercourse. Lady digs me.

I did a flip and landed beside her. A real handful of lady if ever there was one, heroic dimensions, but exquisitely put together, about 38-29-42. What used to be called a "stallion" in some circles.

"Listen, let's go somewhere and talk business," I whispered. Her left eyebrow hooked up when I said "business." I knew I was on the right track.

We casually strolled into the bathroom with our drinks and urges.

"Look," I said to her, closing the bathroom door, "I want to do it to you. I'll give you ten dollars for some."

"Okay," she answered, after she watched me peel a ten spot away from a five. Money has a linguistic system of its own.

We immediately had a complicated situation. She couldn't sit on my lap on the toilet seat or anything like that, she would've crushed my thighs into pancakes.

Ingeniously we discovered that she could bend over and hold onto the bath tub edge and that would do the trick.

Big ruffled peasant skirt gathered up to reveal these incredible columns of flesh. I must've stared at her ass for five minutes before plunging into the core of it all.

71

We surprised each other. I assumed that entering a woman as large as she was would be like wandering into a museum or a supermarket. Her first serious moan and her clenching motion on the tub edge told me that she was getting her money's worth too.

Cold blooded doggie fuck. Her knees were buckling from climaxes when I finally came, one of those 375. Magnum spurts from the back of the head and heels.

My knees were a bit unsteady too, as we toweled our crotches up and prepared to return to the "party." Opening the door for her, I looked back and discovered a puddle of cum on the floor. It was obvious that something extraordinary had been done.

By the next day the whole thing was fading like a sweet dream; I was on to the next movement.

After Rosa had informed me (at least ten times) that Modessa wanted me to call her, I did, finally. The aftermath is what I call the Summer of Modessa and Rosa.

I don't know what it was about that summer, the summer of 1961. Maybe it was the humidity. Or the passionate mood bringing in the '60's. Whatever it was made another kind of summer for me.

We smoked mint flavored weed, ate mint sherbet with Beefeater gin splashed over it and made love, Modessa, Rosa and me, under rose colored lights, juicy shadows sprinkling all over us.

It was a dream summer, one that I will always look back at with pleasure. They allowed me a glimpse of something special, taught me to understand how their love for each other differed from their love for me.

At one point it seemed almost too good and we had to bring another person into the space, to see if what we were experiencing could be validated by a third party.

He thought us a trio of crazed hedonists and we eased him

right on off the set.

In 1961 I was twenty-four years old and some weird stuff began to happen. The U.S. Government was beginning to annoy me a bit. At first I couldn't figure out what they wanted, what with their nasty little notes coming at me from two different directions. They finally got down to the bottom line, they wanted my body.

My ex-wife, the infamous Norma, had set her third dimensional trap; she had informed the proper authorities that we were no longer a couple and they were beginning to need single, Black males, as usual.

Weird shirt. All of a sudden I was being sent these unusual papers to answer and stuff. They were on my ass like white on rice.

I decided to flee. I don't remember the details but, somehow, I made arrangements to absent myself from work and tripped to California. Los Angeles.

My faulty reasoning was that if I got far enough away they'd forget about me. Or if they caught up with me, they'd give me a European vacation.

All of my information on the Army indicated that they did things so ass backwards that if you were on the west coast they'd send you to the east (France or Italy or somewhere) and vice versa.

After about six weeks of living on Figueroa Street, first with Lambert and George, recently arrived-from-Chicago veterans of a peace time bit in Germany, and Herb, my buddy from around the corner on Bowen Avenue, I was beginning to think I had escaped.

Strange lil' period. I didn't have the kind of developed consciousness that said "fuck it." Hell no, I won't go! Like, it wasn't that kind of time. There was no overt war going on. A few tensions here and there but nothing that my head was into. Vietnam was a vague problem, over yonder.

Chapter 8

The bullshit came to a startling halt one morning down on 9th and Broadway. After the sergeant had struggled through a collection of old Hakawabashikawas and Santagenillatosantos and the like, he called out "Hawkins!" and my ass was in the Army.

Officially, on several different levels, it was the most miserable fucking period I can recall in my entire life, up to that moment.

The post office, at the governmental level, in Chicago, had offered the individual an opportunity to do his thang. If you could get away with peddling dope on the eighth floor at midday   fine. If you could get someone/pay someone to punch your card   fine. Whatever it was that you could get away with, fine.

The Army was another level of that kind of thinking. The thing about it is that it was so well disguised that it took me eight weeks of basic training to discover it.

Army, miserably regimented bullshit, incredible learning experience. I actually found out how inefficient our government really is. The Army was/is the ultimate weapon that any government can use to extricate itself from difficulties. Behind that premise are so many problems, contradictions and beaurocratic obstacles that we should feel extremely fortunate that the wars we've had have been fought elsewhere.

Fort Ord wasn't so bad. Fresh ocean air. Seaside, Carmel, bonsai beauty and San Francisco reasonably close, good wholesome chow, characteristically interesting sergeants.

It was like a game. I didn't like marching in line behind dozens of other people, but I liked walking and there was something special about lunch after having been out on the firing range since dawn.

In addition, I'd never been surrounded by so many different characters in my life and that was a trip.

Japanese, Greeks (Defterios, where are you?) Hungarians, Blacks from Honduras and other places where I wasn't even aware that they had Black folks. Indians, weirdos, Jews of all persuasions, freaks, madmen, Turks, Armenians, Bulgarians, name it.

I got off into something called Tae Kwon Do for a couple weeks with an Indonesian dude named Fodran and didn't even know what it was.

The eight week basic training cycle slipped by pretty fast and then, in that peculiar way that dinosaur-headed organizations function, I found myself being flown eastward, to Fort Lee, Virginia, to learn how to build boxes.

The Army had decided I was quartermaster corps material. How? I'll never know.

The idea was to have ten of us attend a three week session of box making and similar classes and shoot us on to our "permanent" assignments.

So damned inefficient, the beaurocracy. Somehow we wound up in Richmond, Virginia five days too soon. No problem, Elchuck and I changed into civvies, stuffed our duffel bags into bus station lockers and proceeded to hitchhike to New York.

Dumb. Really dumb. A Black and a white hitchhiking through Virginia in 1962 was considered a biggie, like certain people would throw moonshine bottles out at you, or circle around and come back to make certain that they had really seen what they had seen. Very dangerous undertaking. We could've been given a lift by the Nazis or the Klan.

Memories   a word or so about Andre Elchuck.

I don't know what he was, Jewish maybe, I can't be certain. Thin dude about five feet eight, thick glasses propped up on a nose that was almost a Semitic caricature, from Canada via California   lots of heart.

We became friendly somehow, I don't remember how. At any rate, the two of us hitchhiked back to Virginia after having had a fuzzy few days in New York.

Fort Lee, Virginia. I wandered into my assigned barracks and heard John Coltrane blowing "My Favorite Things." Despite the heat and the bugs I knew things couldn't be too bad if Coltrane was there.

Murry Norman DePillars, an ex-junior college and post office buddy was there, and a kind of semi-crazed brother from St. Louis, brother named Small, was there. There were a few others, just enough to make a Black Mafia.

We formed a jazzy corner of the barracks and began to ignore the instructions being given concerning the building of boxes. The classes were a real waste of time.

Petersburg ate up the rest of the boredom. This was our spot for the evenings. Or rather, one side of one street (Halifax Street) was our spot for the evenings.

I didn't know from beans about the South. I knew the South-

77

side of Chicago and that my Daddy and his side of the family came from Mississippi, and that Arkansas was my mother's ancestral place but I had no real sense of what the South was.

It was a good thing too, when I think back to it. I was too ignorant to be afraid.

For three sticky weeks DePillars, Small and I tripped to Halifax Street. Sometimes separately, sometimes together.

Elchuck and I remained friendly but we couldn't get into having a social life together. Petersburg, Virginia in 1962 wasn't ready for that.

Halifax Street, eleven fifteen p.m., a kind of Catfish Row atmosphere; barbeque joints, young warriors strolling, trying to catch something before the last bus back to camp.

The period filters back as a steaming dream . . . sleeping through these incredibly dull box building lectures, given by "all-my-life" sergeants mostly Southerners, ("lissen heah") going into town at the end of the Army day, staying in town until three or four in the morning—frantic cab ride back to the post, up at six for the beginning of another lousy-ass day in the Army.

We shot pool in the rec room all night the day before our permanent duty stations were posted on the bulletin board.

Tricky feeling. It was like a gamble, shooting craps with a pair of dice you'd never seen or held in your hand.

Lucky man Murry got sent to Fort Jay, New Yawk. I got sent down south, to Fort Gordon, Georgia. I protested to the little bullet headed lieutenant. I bitched 'n screamed. Georgia? Who in the hell wanted to go to Georgia?!

Not to worry, I was sent anyway.

Memories, Scars . . . Georgia.

Elchuck and me, again. Destiny seemed to be doing a little dance on our heads. He was being exiled too.

Augusta, Georgia. Hot, humid day. We'd just gotten off the train, been taken to the bus station on Broad Street to wait for the next bus to Fort Gordon.

"Hey, Hawk, we got an hour, let's take a look at this dump."

"Yeah, why not?"

I readjusted my heavy ass cap and followed him out of the waiting room. Call it strolling on Broad Street.

August, 1962. Real southern town, filled with real Southerners. Status of "The Confederate Soldier" leaning on his rifle in the middle of Broad Street. Atmosphere thick with serious tensions.

Two blocks from the bus station the Military Police picked us up, took us to the nearest police station and made it super clear that Blacks and whites didn't "fraternize" in Augusta, and especially not Black and white soldiers. We were then escorted back to the bus station and told to wait there for the bus. Period.

I felt a sense of rage that has never left me. The segregation, the racism that I had always experienced in Chicago left you feeling as though you might be able to hang on, survive, get something together, work your way out of it somehow.

This was different, here the gun was at your skull, with no possibility of ducking. I developed a deep respect for my people in the South, after having been made aware of how much closer the gun was to their skulls. Granted, it was a matter of inches, but still

On the bus to the post, watching the town slip from white, affluent, neat, clean to dusty, crusty, disorderly, Black; I made a silent resolution to remain on post for the remaining twenty months for my servitude.

I held out for three

Memories . . . scars

They had shuffled me into the 92nd Civil Affairs Group, which meant that me and an assorted bunch of hillbillies, wops and weirdos would've been responsible for setting up a civilian government if the U.S. decided to take Cuba back.

Or try to wipe Vietnam off the world. An elite unit in other words.

Our Civil Affairs Group was, oddly thinking, a definite reflection of our society. Mainly meaning a bunch of crazed people.

If we had ever had to deal with the possibility of dealing with the establishment of a government, ain't no telling what these fools would've come up with.

They were fucked up, the whole bunch. Klansmen with Confederate flags stuck up inside their lockers, shit on their minds so weird that you'd have to be a white, a psychiatrist or a Black man with a survival level of ten, to understand their garbled up personalities.

I had a dude in the bunk next to me named Woodrum who used to snore, stink, get drunk, talk sloppy and lose his money on "fast wimmen," dice and funny cards. He was guilty of the sort of behavior that he and his buddies used to attribute to "nigguhs." Matter of fact, Woodrum was one of the most representative "nigguhs" I'd ever met.

We/us all Black people, even the upper grade chevron holders, were an army within the Army. It was deep, down there in Georgia.

I was a buck private but one of my best friends was a career soldier from the Virgin Islands. We couldn't afford the privilege of trying to outrank each other. Blacks were going through too much as a group to section ourselves off from each other. There were, of course, the usual exceptions.

The Establishment considered me a dud.

"Gollydamnit Hawkins! you ain't never gonna make it in this man's army!" Sergeant Roughnuts.

I could've been a superior soldier if I had wanted to, if I had let them do it to me. I was determined that I would not let them do it to me.

My real attitude was uncovered too soon for my comfort.

I don't know   there just seemed to be something completely and utterly fucked up about being asked to serve, to pay attention to all the neat lil' pieces of military bullshit when we couldn't even go into certain places, even in uniform. It was a real big crock of merde to me and I wasn't having any.

For three long months I read books, took long walks, went to all of the post movies, played drums at the service clubs. I did everything but go to town.

My friends understood what was happening and left me alone. Three months is a bunch of dull evenings on a military post.

Memories   no scars.

Amazon of a brown-skinned woman. I'll have to do a bit of psycho work on this lil' dude/big lady syndrome. Amazonic.

Whatever her name was/is, Amazonic should be added somewhere.

Long corridors, the base hospital was attached to our barracks area by long corridors. Weird arrangement. You could walk through a hslf mile of corridors before reaching our area.

These incredibly long corridors were maintained by Black people from the town. They swept, scrubbed, waxed, dusted, emptied ash pails, they worked hard.

The Amazonic sister was one of the labor force. A beautifully warm smile opens up in front of me, no name, just a beautifully warm smile and the softly slurred words, "why you lookin' so mean?"

I must have been carrying a full pound of cheese on my chest by this time, I mean, like, as some folks would say, I was really "horny."

I managed to make it my business to be where I knew she would be for the next couple days. She prompted me to unclench my jaws, to smile. We talked about the differences between Blacks in the North and Blacks in the South.

She thought I was strangely funny. We made a date to get together after work. It was on a Friday

Bus load of Black working class folks returning to the compound after having spent a day on the plantation. Somehow it seemed that everyone on the bus knew something about what we were up to.

I'll call her "My Lady." My Lady was an ex-Wac with a large, good time loving family. Uncles with grey, grizzled senses of time and humor, aunts full of lascivious attitudes and a stream of inners and outers who just simply wanted to see who the lil' soldier boy was. I fell into 'em like a duck into water, they were my people.

After a couple six packs of something and a couple pints of cheap whiskey (everything was cheaper in 1962) we were into each other.

She whispered some secretive magic words to her sister and the next thing I knew, after we had wandered through some piney smelling woods for a few hundred yards, we were undressing in a log cabin. A log cabin! with newspapers plastered into the cracks. A log cabin!

Beautiful lady, beautiful scene. Fragrant wood burning in the fireplace beside our bed, us doing some heroic fuckin', My Lady and me.

"Do what you want to do, baby," she slurred into my ear. And I tried.

She was deepest Black Georgia, red running Earth, Black Goodness, honey on the dick, soul sweet and I had a three month old sweet tooth.

An hour later, after we fell over into a sexual slag heap and dreamily watched the log fire die down to charcoals, I felt a euphoria that I knew would only be repeated a few times in my life. I was certain of it. And it's been true.

My Lady saved me from Georgia, the Georgia that I had thought of, the world that represented Crackerdom, was undermined by people from another place.

I mentally kicked my ass a thousand times after that night. If we had been able to do our own immense Black thang in Chicago, on the South and Westside, what the hell had made me believe that the same set of circumstances wouldn't be true in the South?

Our Northern white boy spoke in a different dialect (several of them, as befitting a forked tongue) and so did theirs. My personal satori was somewhat shitty, I should've known better.

After My Lady it was me and Georgia. I never saw her after that night and sometimes, after the influence of too much creative input, I imagined that she had not been real, perhaps a Circe, or an Iyalosa sent to save me.

Me and Georgia meant that I had surrendered to evenings and weekends with my friends. Jack Kidd, Elroy Steele (from the Virgin Islands) Thomas McKinnon. Rich Strongheart, Gordon Bussey (the two hundred fifty pound intellectual from Bed-Sty) Maxwell (from a small place in Florida) and a precious few others.

We were precious and few and we made ourselves mean something to each other. We were brothers.

Jack Kidd from Eula, Georgia, did the heaviest number of my head, in a manner of speaking. Being from Georgia (in Georgia) he understood a bunch of stuff that some of us outsiders missed.

In a way, Georgia was something like the first real down-south country I had visited since Mexico.

After I got off into it a bit, Georgia was a lot like Mexico. The whites were in control, the mestizos were unhappy and disturbed and the "Indians" were in a mood to brutalize the whole setup, demands forced into being by the whole abnormal set up. Who said white people should rule anything?

In any case, I wasn't spending all my time up on the post

anymore. I was tripping out, doing wild stuff. Some evenings, if we didn't have any duties, we'd leave the post and party hearty until an hour before reveille. Many times, I strolled into the barracks in a zombied state, changed into my greenish shit and stood in formation to be counted, feeling exactly like a zombie.

In a way, except for my evil attitude, I *was* a zombie. The "master" had control of my body and my salute but circumstances had control of the rest of me. It was a unique state to be in.

Sunday morning in the Tasty Shoppe. Me and Steele are hung-strung over after a Friday and Saturday of boozin', bitchin' 'n whoopin' it up   remember?

Beautiful woman, Georgia gorgeous, low yaller lady in basic black, a strand of pearls circling her gorgeous throat, with a beautiful lil' Black daughter.

I saw them drive up and park in the lot across the street. What would a woman like this one be doing in the Tasty Shoppe? Not that I mean to put the Tasty Shoppe down by any means. The Tasty Shoppe was where it was!

A small army of soulful Black middle-aged sisters off in the kitchen, swelling biscuits up and making puddings 'n doing other things that were so outrageously good that there was nothing to do but eat and moan. Lois Dwan, James Beard and the rest of them would've had gastronomic orgasms at the Tasty Shoppe. Good restaurant.

R.S. and her daughter stroll in. Steele, an Army cook, of all things, is bent so far off into his sausage, grits 'n eggs, that he doesn't notice anything.

I notice. The lady is fine, lush, in only that way that Black women can be lush. She glances at me, I stare at her. Her daughter skips past me to put a nickel (a nickel!) in the record player. I recode her with a quarter, obviously a kid used to being spoiled.

The daughter takes a note back to a mother filled with sexuality, from a soldier filled with lust. Mother looks soulfully at the soldier, gives him her phone number and nods. Ahhhhhhhhh

Sunday afternoon, more drinking, more story telling. By twilight I find myself asking myself, what the hell is all this about? Time to escape, call this lady who gave me her number this morning in the Tasty Shoppe. Let's see what that's about.

Brazilian 'phone call, off rhythms. "Yeas, c'mon, my mother's here."

Perilous trip. After a few minutes, my only clear notion of things, was that he was delivering the straight to the Grand Dragon.

After a few more minutes, I was absolutely certain of it. I was scared.

What do you say to a redneck, turkey buzzard lookin' cab driver, who seems to know where he's going?

He delivered me to the proper spot, above and past my prayers. I had no sincere belief that he was taking me to the right place; the people in Chicago (that I had been intimate with, had never had grass in their front yard, or lanterns) had planted a professional sense of racial understanding in my mind about white cab drivers. And here I was, in Georgia, of all places, being delivered to the right spot.

I paid him, being reassured all the while that I was in the right place.

"You sure this is the right place?"

"Yeah. This here's the rat place."

Black suburb in Georgia, complete with gaslit lamps, a different trip altogether.

R.S. welcomed me, her mother whipped another brew into my hand and after a decent interval, eased off into the bedroom with the lil' girl.

I'll never know how we did it, what kind of chemistry ignited the process, all I know is this; one minute we were sitting on the sofa in this beautifully furnished home and the next minute I was gently helping her unthread her thighs through her panties.

Scene: The television is on, up just loud enough to mask our low moans, a man is struggling up a sand dune, really struggling.

It's true, what the old people used to say about the stolen melon being the sweetest. It was sweet.

The history began to surface. R.S.' husband had wrapped himself around a lamp pole the year before I met her leaving her money in the bank, a home, a car, insurance money, a daughter and a rare passion for fucking.

My grizzled little Chicago-street-poisoned mind flicked at dirty thoughts like a snake's tongue on the way back to camp.

The setup was perfect. She was just the right age (thirty-six), just the right state of ripeness for everything. I was smiling, for the first time since I'd been dumped in Georgia.

I was really bad for R.S. At that point I could righteously say that I was bad for myself. I would've been bad for anybody.

I hated being held captive, locked up, the regimentation, the stupid sergeant, the hillbillies. I could nut out and say that I took my frustrations out on her, but that would only be half true.

I discovered the high and low places of Augusta, Georgia. There were women in the clubs, the boody shakers and good timers. And there was the library, but first the women in the clubs.

There were only three public "night clubs" in Augusta's African-American sector in 1962, the De Soto, the Top Hat and the Paramount. Butterfly McQueen of *Gone With the Wind* fame worked as a barbeque cook for a time in the Paramount.

I don't recall what a prostitute looked like in Augusta. What with all the soldiers, one would think that they would've been swarming all over the place, but they weren't.

The thing to do, I was told before I realized that I had it going on already, was to grab hold of a lady and form a two-some. Or a threesome if she had a child.

Shacking up was what it was called, but it represented more than just a casual sexual setup. It was stable and gave the woman P.X. privileges.

I fell head over buttermilk with the Black southern female. Lush ladies, resilient, tough, brainy, more nerves than a brass assed monkey, full of warmth and strength.

Of course it doesn't make any sense to make regional distinctions between women, but I just did.

Coming from the sisters in Chicago who had to keep an eye out for the approaching winter, and all of what that would mean, was piss poor preparation for southern sisters who seemed ready to bankrupt themselves with every lovely adjective and gesture.

I had no preparation for Ella either. The librarian in the Gwinnet Street branch; a soft, pale beige with green-grey eyes, oceans of dimples at each corner of her mouth, finely put together, not too much anywhere, but all there. I started going to the library a lot.

It was a rich experience, those two years. So much was happening at one time; I would grind my way through an Army day, hating the stupid beaurocracy that forced us to get up so early for no sensible reason, other than to stand at attention in the chilled dawn while somebody shouted, "All present and accounted for, sir!" Dumb shit. And the racism, the all pervasive racism.

And finally, as soon as I could sneak away (assuming I hadn't been cornered by some idiotic "duty") I would be off to town.

A brief stop in the library, to exchange pleasantries with a woman I was gradually learning to love. And then, if she were at work, a stroll down the street to R.S.' job (medical technician of some kind, talked about assisting with operations) to get the car.

A drink with the brothers in the De Soto. Or a date with a startlingly dark brown-skinned lady that I had met three days before.

It went that way for a goodly number of months, interwoven with leaves to Chicago.

I was home on a two week leave when I met Billie. It's a wonder I had a chance to see anybody, outside of the little room that I had rented in the Avon for two weeks of lascivious behavior.

Du Sable High School was having a reunion, the class of '55, I think. A bunch of old friends gathered in the Parkway Ballroom to have sly chitchat and see who had gotten far, that sort of number. I went with my partner, George. Just a lark, nothing better to do.

I should've known Billie, from circling each other in some of the same neighborhoods, but I didn't. We had simply circled each other, knowing other people that knew us but not each other.

Billie was a beautiful Black woman then and, if she's alive now, even more beautiful. You could see that in her, way back then.

Small boned, very Indian looking (Hindu or Pakistani) lovely, like a flower. The analogy ends there, there was nothing fragile about her.

I stared at her, mesmerized by her energetic movements (I was surprised to learn that she had worked at her mother's restaurant before coming to the reunion) a little bit hypnotized by her beauty.

After the reunion, an after set at Bill Mitchell's house. Billie winds up sitting between George and me (I had insisted she ride with us) on a small sofa. I proceeded to rap.

I rapped my way into a marriage that night. The marriage didn't take place 'til a couple years later but we laid the carpet leading to it that night.

Crazy feeling   it started off as a semi-test of gamesmanship between George and me. Billie, acting as the good natured referee, nodding sweetly to both of us, and suddenly, without the slightest signal offering us any notice of the changeover, we became serious.

I'm sure I told her I loved her that night, amongst other things. I think I would've told her anything I thought she wanted to hear   that's how badly I wanted her.

It was dawn before I stopped talking. The die was cast. Somehow we were going to get something together.

I was feverish about Billie. It was like the first time I'd ever been in love. There were other considerations too. I had one daughter that I knew about (living with my mother) and she had two daughters. We could form a lovely "political" marriage, it was going to be sweet.

I returned to Georgia after two weeks of Billie, jellied up by her presence in my life. I sniffed her perfume on the one page letters she wrote me. I longed and lusted for her.

It was a wonderfully complex time. I was in love with Ella and Billie.

It would be difficult for me to put my finger on the moment, but it would seem that someone took note of my wonderfully new attitude and decided to do something about it. Don't tell me sergeants don't think.

In one cunningly fierce move, I was "offered" the job of/as fireman for the 95th Civil Affairs Unit. Simple job, really. All I had to do was keep all of the hot water heaters hot. That was the summer time part of it . . . just keeping the water hot.

It was considered the dead beat detail. Firemen were on

duty twenty-four hours and were supposed to have twenty-four hours off. The penalty for being derelict on duty was slyly unexplained but understood, the stockade, bad time, serve six months, come out and start over where you left off. It was a bit like being in debt to the company store.

Winter came in hard and cold. I began shoveling coal in earnest now. The rotten bastards! I shoveled coal to heat four barracks and three office buildings. I worked my twenty-four (and sneaked away to nap, from time to time) and when I was supposed to be getting off duty, they'd always have some extra piece of shit for me to do that someone else should've done. Seven months on the coal pile from seven in the morning until seven in the morning again, every other day for seven months.

I'm sure I went a little crazy, measuring the steps from one barrack's furnace to another, slamming two heaping shovels full of coal into the fires.

I stand in front of the furnace, feeling sorry for myself and murderous. The rest of the people are upstairs asleep, warmed in the night by my efforts. I stare into the furnace and wonder what it would feel like to be a flame.

Dazzling faces sometimes pulled me to the lips of the furnace doors and spoke to me. One night a voice asked me to pull off my clothes and cuddle up next to it. It was only the ambiguous hermaphrodictic qualities of the voice that saved me, I couldn't tell whether a male or female wanted me. I hesitated and then resisted.

I was coated with black coal dust, I was black black black. An Untouchable.

In addition, I still had to make inspections (which meant working ten times harder to get clean) and perform my other "soldierly" duties, as determined by the person in charge. They tried to break my spirit and failed. The dirty rotten motherfuckers!

Coldbloodedly they worked my ass until the day before my discharge and, would you beleive? tried to do fun 'n games with me on my discharge day.

"You know, you done done enough stuff for us to hold on to you a while longer?"

It was supposed to be some kind of version of a sergeant's joke but it wasn't funny to me.

Poor R.S. I received my "walking papers" at eleven a.m. and I was on the train to Chicago by two that afternoon; the khaki nightmare was over.

It was a rotten way to do someone who had been so kind, generous and loving to me, a really rotten way. I didn't even write her a note to tell her I was leaving.

Chapter 9

Back to the Post Office. The government still had me by the short hairs.

Sister sitting next to me in Illinois section says, "You act like you just got out of the Army."

"Why do you say that?"

"Well, cause you so quiet, they usually real quiet when they just got back here from the Army."

It was more than a quiet for me, I was stunned. There I was, back in the post office, with all the dust, the brutal noise, the madness of the scene. It was as though none of it had ever happened   Georgia—two years, 1962-64—a rich chapter there.

Back to the Avon, to sew it up with Billie. God! she had my nose wide open! But that didn't stop me from being my usual hedonistic self

The Avon was still parties and celebrations. Never lived

in a place that was so full of life. But, as is usual in life, changes do occur. Families had come to the Avon.

When the building had been full of men, the noises floating out of the rooms had been solidly sexual and sensual, now there was domestic discord, arguments and groans, not moans. But the overwhelming majority of signals were still pleasurable.

It was a mad mad time. Billie had shown me that she was in my corner by flying down to meet me in Atlanta over the course of a three day pass. And she had loaned me some money. And she was beautiful. What more could I ask for?

1964, the winter of that year.

Billie would leave her mother's restaurant after a ten or twelve hour day, come to my room in the Avon with a platter of cold chicken or whatever.

Sometimes we made ethereal love but more often we held each other closely and made vague plans for a future.

My daughter was still staying with my mother and that was a situation that I knew I'd have to do something about.

Aside from that, I felt more than the urge to be with Billie; I was deeply in love with her and I wanted her to share my piece of life.

Things were going along beautifully until I goofed. Weird how it happened. A couple buddies had taken me around the corner to the Mayflower Hotel, to meet one of them's sister and a couple of her girlfriends.

Ola was one of his sister's girlfriends. Ola from Oklahoma. Never will forget her. Ola and I took a walk to my room in the Avon. I don't know why, we just did. Warm, semi-humid, Chicago summer day.

Ola was very pretty. Half Comanche/half Afro-Caribbean, tawny colored, real fine lady.

We sat in my room and chitchatted about an hour and slowly strolled back to the Mayflower Hotel. Somehow we had set the stage, we knew something was going to come off.

Party was happening in the building that evening. That very evening, and Billie was scheduled to put in an appearance, which was something I had completely forgotten about.

Like most of the minor league seductionists in the building I had installed a cool blue light to focus on my amorous doings

Keep your eye on that light and see what happens

Wild party! a bunch of West Indian-Africans had recently moved into the building and they knew how to git down!

Funk ridden scene, sweat glands open, asses twirling in sugar bun spirals, fleshy buttocks melting into Black basketball-sized hands, drum melodies, sensuality mammy, Jamaican rum, mon.

Ola and I caught each other's expressions and eased away to my room. We strolled into the room, measured the distance to each other and oozed out of our clothes and into each other. It was coldblooded action.

After about fifteen minutes of something that was threatening to go beyond mere sex, what with the music and sound orgy coming through the door, Ola and I settled down into a bit of oceanic fucking. She was sexual magic. I'll leave it at that.

Finally, at high tide, it ended, whatever it had been, and both of us fell over in a slow motion heap, completely crazed from what we had done together.

For a day and a night we lay in this heap, played out, panting and then the music seemed to fade behind the knocking knocking on the door. Billie.

I had forgotten about her, Ola had reinforced my forgetfulness. Billie

Memories

In just the same way that things have happened like that since the start, time was suspended. Ola, genius, understood

95

the whole business with a coldly vicious smile, stood and redressed lightening quick, comb-fluffed her hair and opened the door while my good friend Felt was trying to convince Billie that he had seen me trip down the stairs a few minutes ago.

Ola, beautiful Ola, edged past Billie, gently excusing herself. Billie stalks into the room, steam blowing out of her nostrils and ears, picks up a few odds 'n ends that had accumulated during the course of our love affair and stomped out. I was crushed.

I had gone from high tide to being blasted against the rocks in an hour. Ola, Ola, Ola; I sometimes wonder why she did that but, since I never saw her again, I never had a chance to ask.

Billie baby forced me to put on some serious knee pads, like pay penance, before she gave me another chance. She was cold-cold-coldblooded.

She'd make a solemn promise to meet with me, to discuss things, and wouldn't show. She simply lied to me, coldly.

I lost weight and had bad dreams. I wanted her love and respect more than anything I could think of. It was an uphill struggle but the bottom line found us living together on 71st and Stoney Island. I had looked all over the city to come up with a place big enough for the five of us.

For the second time in my young life I became a family man. I was a good and sometimes a bad family man but I was an excellent father.

I loved and still love my children. Despite the fact that Erika was mine and Sarita and Jackie weren't, made no difference. I saw them as young individuals who needed direction and guidance.

Family man? No, not really. There was so much love in the world for me to just love one woman. And she expected that.

One night I decided to break out of the shell, start life off in a different place, go west to California. It happened almost like that.

An urge to evade another Chicago winter had a lot to do with me making the decision, that, and that peculiar notion that California might be far enough away from the "United States" to make me forget the worst of what Georgia had done to me. Chicago was too much of a reminder, minus magnolia blossoms.

A neat little fever took hold of my brain. I applied for a transfer to Los Angeles and, within a few months the beaurocracy had found a way.

I hadn't spoken to many people about the move. So, one night after work, standing around outside the Post Office, when I dropped the news that I was leaving, wouldn't be back in the Post Office no mo', everybody just stared at me and smiled that smile.

A couple weeks later I cut out, patiently explaining to Billie and my children that I would send for them within a short time.

I didn't know how long it would take to save a stake after I started work, to rent a place, etc. I knew people in Los Angeles but I didn't know shit about living in Los Angeles.

I was taking a potentially disastrous gamble but I felt it was necessary. The thought in the back of my skull was—hell! if I'm going to live here, why not live on the Riviera and not in Siberia.

When I left I had the feeling that Billie never expected to see me again.

The beaurocracy played its usual little crazy game with me. For some reason I discovered after my arrival that I wouldn't be able to start working for six weeks.

I had counted on continuing my paychecks and slipping Billie and the kids onto the scene by the third week. That was not to be.

A lil' money in pocket staying with Herb and Mamie, killing time in the sun until my timecard arrived. Or whatever they were transferring from the Chicago Post Office.

Herb, noble friend, gave me the use of a huge grey Cadillac that he had nicknamed, "The Grey Ghost."

A whole pile of stuff happened during the course of that span of time. Number one, I got fed up with listening to, feeling the tensions that operated between the couple.

It got so bad I had to git on. I picked up my diddy bag, tripped over to 115th and Figueroa and rented an apartment. It was the winter of 1966 and it was *cold*.

It seems, at times, that I can trace certain periods, certain feelings and developments back to certain rooms.

I was going the economy route with my apartment taking. I made a decision to have no gas bill, no light bill, no telephone bill, nothing that would prevent me from saving money.

I remember Palmer coming by one sunny afternoon, asking me to, "leave the door open, Hawk, let some heat come in."

It was on the west side of the street and, what with the shadows and chill bumps, it was always cool in the day and cold as hell at night. It also rained a lot that winter, a cold, vicious rain that kept my apartment permanently dank.

It was an interesting period, very definitely romantic. The Beverly Hills Post Office finally worked my status out with the Chicago Post Office. I was back on the clock.

I also started to write, seriously. I'd come into my ice palace of an evening, light a candle, put on all the shirts I had, crawl up in bed (covered by donated blankets) and start scribbling. There's no telling what was coming out of me, if anything, but I was doing it, I was writing.

I was alone and I dealt with it. I can't say I really liked it but I dealt with it.

Finally, raking and scraping it together, I was able to rent a tiny small apartment on 103rd and Avalon and proceed to go about the business of living.

While the three girls slept on a Murphy bed in the front room, Billie and I made love every night for nine days on an inflated camp mattress on the kitchen floor.

The rhetoric of Blackness hadn't become fully blown up at the time, it didn't have to be for me, I loved my Black woman to distraction, along with all of the other women I loved.

It was working out. We had transformed our family into a group of sunshinists, we were on the coast. The thing to do was find ourselves.

Mrs. Brown, the soft brown sister with New York brains, will always be a favorite person in my life, the person who rented us the house on 89th and Menlo.

89th and Menlo, a couple blocks from the shopping area on Manchester and Vermont.

It was nice, all of it. Billie had friends from Chicago living in Compton. I was working at the Beverly Hills Post Office and things looked reasonably rosy. Only problem was that I was not happy with the situation. It was strange, I didn't know what it was but I knew something wasn't.

One day, on what I thought was an impulse, I decided to quit working at the post office. Somehow, the more I thought about it, it seemed stupid to be working inside while most of California was outside.

I put in my resignation, not having the slightest notion of what I wanted to do, let alone where I wanted to go. It was cracker jack action time, no telling what might pop out of the box.

Billie thought I was mad, I know she did. I have the memories of enough telephone conversations to remember that, her talking to people about me.

Three children to feed, rent to pay, a real raggedy car, the whole avocado, I had it. I recognized that all I'd have to do was keep a low profile and gradually, gradually I'd become a
whatever it was that one became under the circumstances.

After a few days of governmental unemployment, I *panicked* and they resupplied me with a job that would've/should've been fine. I wound up working at the Veterans Administration as a mail clerk-messenger. Stupid job. You were supposed to memorize mail-message delivery routes; the place was a gigantic Quanset "hut" with God only knows how many offices in it, like a goddamned maze.

I tripped through the place doing every strange thing I could think of. I kiss-fondled-romanced one of the local Foreign Legionnaires (Veterans of Foreign Wars, Amerrikkkan branch) daughter, a really clean cut Irish lass who was fed up with her father's overpowering urge to commit incest. Seems that I was beginning to break away from things, strictures I didn't even know about that had been holding me in place.

I took an objective look at the person I was married to and decided that the whole thing was pure bullshit.

We were incompatible, the only thing we really had going for us was the kids and a sense of romance. The problem was that the romance had to do with what *was*, not for what was current.

I loved Billie but I recognized that it was not going to be possible to git down with her. She was from a place that stressed security, stability, complacency. Nothin' wrong with any of that, with all of that, except that I knew, after awhile, that it wasn't for the kid. Feeding on that realization, I got crazy and started doing really radical shit.

Memories

Thunderous rainy night; I have been sitting up at our dining room table scribbling. I couldn't honestly call it writing because I didn't know what I was doing. There was no real form to my method. It was just simply a dude taking his frustration out on paper.

After a bit, I pushed the paper to the side, hung the pencil up and strolled out into the rain. I circled the block and walked through the muddy alley behind our street, awakening every barking dog in the neighborhood as I made my moves.

I hopped over the fence at the rear of our house and popped into the back door of the lady who lived in the little house behind us.

It was all mentally pre-arranged, she was going to be an active catalyst in my plan to dissolve my marriage. I wanted to get caught fucking off. I didn't get caught   well, not actually.

The Veterans Administration was driving me crazy. I'd go to work loaded, take a break at ten fifteen and trip off with the other drug abusers and then it'd be time for lunch. Crazy time.

I was on the down slope, going sideways, when Mrs. C. and I met.

Memories

West Indian type sister, (I don't know, she just seemed to be) with longish arms, a wide, full, delicious mouth, seriously sexy eyes. But that wasn't it, what was it was the sister's hips. Sister had an absolutely exquisite behind. One couldn't call it an ass. It was a *Behind*, it was a sculptured field of action, a transcended mediation. And she was almost aware of it.

Me, dizzily failing out of my family groove. Her husband, a Black version of a crazy white boy was positioned in the Gulf of Tonkin or somewhere like that   1968, Vietnam Time.

We stalked, we talked. We chitchatted. And finally we met, off the premises, in a manner of speaking.

A truly beautiful sister. Sensitive, intelligent, aware. We jumped into a heavyweight sexualistic drama. Being as crazed as I was at the time I don't know what I told Billie to excuse myself for a weekend, I don't even know if I even made up an excuse at all.

Mrs. C. and I are going up to San Francisco on a Sears credit card. Modern/old fashioned lady, the man pays for the trip. Right?

I paid for that one. A rare trip. Some kind of raggedy ass Chevy. Real raggedy. I didn't even know where the motor was. No money except a bit. We/I drove up 101, counting on coming across enough Sears gas pumps to get there and back. Real crazed shit. Fortunately, since the gods smile on drunks and fuckers, we made it there and back.

It's really a wonder that we made it outside the Los Angeles city limits.

Backing up on Mrs. C. for a moment. The decision/*Decision* was made in the Pied Piper one afternoon. I persuaded her to meet me for a drink. Her old man had been away for a year; a moral sister, hadn't even thought about adultery but had never stopped taking birth control pills . . . ahhhem . . .

Soft, balmy lighting, efficient cocktail hostess, slick.

After three gin 'n tonics apiece we were about ready to solve all of the sexual problems anyone could dream of. Off we wanderlust, to a Crenshaw Boulevard motel.

Memories

I looked behind me as we tried to complete a nonchalant stroll from room number seven, back to our car. The scene that I glanced back on was one of total devastation. The bedside lamp had been kicked over by a whirling motion that we'd become fond of, in mid-stroke. The mattress had slipped halfway off the bed, the door even seemed to be ajar at a weird angle. Had we torn it off of its hinges going on?

Mrs. C. and I had discovered each other.

Meanwhile, using animalistic cunning, I had reasoned out that Billie was not going to offer me an out based on sexual indiscretions. I had to do something else.

What would happen if I could convince her that I never fully intended to get off into *money?* Maybe that would work. I tried it and it worked, but it was a process.

One day, with Mrs. C. as a transitional ghost, I quit the Veterans Administration and became a busboy in the Beverly Hills Hotel, in the employees cafeteria; that's in the basement.

Billie, always having suspected me of being slightly out of sync, was now absolutely certain of her suspicions.

From a nice reliable gig in the Post Office to busboy in the employee's cafeteria in the Beverly Hilton, was too much for the sister.

Billie tripped out on me, she had no choice but to divorce me. I was so happy I cried.

Chapter 10

Matters began to flower. I was walking past the Balboa Theater, (on 89th and Vermont) which was being turned into PASLA (Performing Arts Society of Los Angeles) under the heroic direction of Vantile Whitfield, Black theatrical genius incarnate, and asked, "what can I do?"

I was invited to participate. I wound up painting the lobby of the theatre. I got involved with the drama of drama. I was tuned in, turned on. It was almost a holy time for me.

Briefly, having nowhere else to go, I lived on stage.

My days with beautiful Billie over, final divorce papers pending, I moved into an L-shaped room in Compton, took a city civil service exam and passed it—Lawdy! Lawdy!

Now what?

I was a probationery janitor, working whenever they notified me that I should be. It was truly and fuckingly absolutely wonderful.

For the first time since I was an adult male individual, I was Free!

I had a place to live, the L-shaped room (more on that later), I had something to do   Live! and I could write whenever the urge was on me. What else could I possibly want?

As a county custodian, I got to know the various welfare offices around town. Well, not really to know them but to know their floors and a few of the social workers, at any rate.

One day I'd be 'way over somewhere, stripping 'n waxing a hundred yards of floor, next day I'd be working with some other people in another place, picking up the larger scraps of paper. Cold-blooded gig, from four to twelve, with about three whole hours worth of work up in there someplace.

And a whole bunch of other intrigue. Example: supervisor, high yaller skinned Black woman, who found herself amazed to be talking with a custodian about her trip to Mexico City. Shit! I'd been there in 1959 with crazy ass Norma.

Kind of an oddly rhythmed Black lady with a beautiful yellow Jag, sexually active but not sexually inclined. Spooky was the word for her.

Mrs. C., there too. I can't honestly say what she saw in me, especially since she knew as well as I did that sexual glorification was the beginning and ending of our script.

Scars

The Compton Courthouse, sweeping and mopping out the holding tank. You could image what the day had been like in the holding tank from the lingering perfume, the rank stink of fear.

It was all there

I was living in the L-shaped room when PASLA, having manufactured itself into an artistic entity under Van, decided to have a costume ball.

The theme was "Primitives of the World." Some of the

white folks involved came in Lapp outfits, completely on the other side of the Arctic.

It was nice, the whole thing. Towards the end I met Jeanngy. Lady was standing near one of the pillars in the ballroom of the Hilton. I had not "caught" and was feeling the worse for it.

Jeanngy took a few words from my vocabulary and decided that I was a writer.

Funny scene, to me, my room with a shadow-stage bed-in-front-of-a-window must've been my neighborhood's sexual side show. And there was a serious Baptist church across from me.

I didn't know what could be seen from inside the damn place until one night, a hot summer night, I watched my friend Jimmy the Dealer and his tall Black woman make love.

I stood down on the sidewalk, studying all the shadowy activity. All I could think of was how many times my neighbors must've applauded my performances. Or booed, depending on the time of day/night, my partner and the state of things.

Meanwhile, with Jeanngy, there was a prophetic weekend. She was into being ethereal, deep. For a weekend that was alternately rained on and shined on, she explained me to myself and went off, back to her usual place, wherever that was. She told me she was a space traveler.

Memories

The L-shaped room in Compton, on Laurel Street, was a moment of pure pleasure. A dour Slav from Alaska owned the place and a very interesting spot on this Earth it was too.

Second floor, entrance on the west side via a fire escape; slick brother in room number one. Real slick, like he'd steal your pension check.

The town's quietest, most fucked up couple in number two, Betsy and Derek. White folks, she with porcelained skin and orange hair, he trips about in pretend-slave anklets and red and black striped pants because that is his natural garb. They are supposed to be hiding out because he is a draft dodger and she is an adolescent runaway.

Later on, they had nerve enough to move into an apartment directly behind the Compton police station and, to compound the madness, grow a few raggedly ass marijuana plants. Weird couple.

I had made a moral commitment to myself to keep Billie supplied with as much money as I could, to maintain.

And I was doing it.

Meanwhile, I was running a sexual circus. One evening it would be the supervisor of this social workers' unit, a middle-aged sister with a dash of Tabasco-nymph in her mind set.

Mrs. C. would whip through, devastating both of my testicles as often as I could stand the erections. Diverse and assorted types of women of high and low repute. It was mellow. And also, at times, a bit frenzied.

And then, in the middle of it, I met M. Impossible to tell how some people are going to come into your life. Best thing to do is stay loose, unprepared.

A brother named Spinks and I worked together at the welfare office on Holmes and Gage doing the barest minimum of what had to be done. Sometimes, for days at a time, we'd only pick up the very largest scraps of paper and empty the trash cans.

It wasn't a bad job at all. I mean, it wasn't the sort of job that you took home with you every night.

Spinks was one of a number of characters I worked with. Brother had real bad feet and a very good heart. Real bad feet. His corns were so bad he actually spent a lot of his time mincing along on his heels. Real bad corns.

Most of the time, when he didn't have his bunions propped up on one of the desks, talking about some woman he'd just fucked to smithereens, or his bookie, he'd be talking about some woman he was going to have. The good brother supplied me with enough lascivious stories to last forever. That's right, forever.

And when he wasn't telling cum-stained fairy tails, he was smoking marijuana. I smoked some PCP lace herb with him one evening and didn't even know it.

"Spinks, what kinda weed is this, it smells strange."

"It's got some PCP on it."

"PCP, what's that?"

"It's some stuff that'll get you higher quicker."

Off brand type dude. He never freaked out or anything but instinct warned me against the continued use of his brand of dope.

"Hawk, you want some o' this?"

"Uhhh, naw, thanks man, I'm gonna stay with this gin."

I had no problem recognizing M. It would've been pretty hard not to recognize her, as unique as she was/is, in a setting as prosaic as that one. It seemed that there were two people in the place who were really out of place she 'n me.

All of the reasons I was out of place are detailed here, her situation was something else. Firstly, she sat in a chair. Everyone else had office chairs, impersonal structures of metal and economy.

She sat in a throne-chair, upholstered in leather, studded with big gleaming tacks, smoking Benson and Hedges and drinking Coca-Colas.

Unusual looking woman. White, but not gleamingly Swiss white or any of those purely pale colors. She was Scotch swarthy (and I defy the shit out of anyone beyond Robert Burns and haggis to relate to that color).

Doing all of the things I was doing, I didn't really relate to who she was and where she was, beyond a certain point. I mean, it was like my own lil ole life was at such a fluttery

109

point (at first) that I couldn't imagine certain things beyond a certain point.

What did I do, with my limited imagination at work? I invited her to go see Hugh Masekela with me at the Whiskey A Go-Go or somewhere. My guess was that a date to dig Hugh would tell me everything I needed to know.

We never made it to the Hugh Masekela set, but we did check out a bunch of other scenes—Ravi Shankar in Copenhagen, Armando Peraza (helping Cal Tjader get his act together) a whole bunch of times, Chili Moran in Mexico City, people and places that became a part of our history to each other.

I didn't really, honestly, know where I was. Half of me was on my job but then there was another part of me that was rationed off into nothing. Have to call it that because that's what it seemed to be.

I was drawn to M. but leery; after all, she *was* white and I had already lost a championship part of my psyche with a bad white woman. I didn't see the slightest need to take on another possible crazy.

In addition, I was really just flirting around mostly. I started off with little notes and sly comments.

Meanwhile, there was this exotic selection of ladies tripping through my L-shaped room. Mrs. C., a semi-mysterical woman with a yellow Jag, (she always peeked out of the window during her two hours with me), one member of a set of twins, ladies from PASLA (the community theater on Vermont Avenue), etc., etc.

I was happy in that little room. Sometimes I can place my finger on exactly what it was that was making me happy. I think the primary source of my joy was the fact that I was alone. The people came and went but I stayed, alone.

Strangely, I can't remember writing very much, a few stray poems, idea stuff, scribbling.

I got lucky enough to get a permanent custodial gig in the Comptom Courthouse, just around the corner from my room

    it was a sweetheart setup. I could walk through a church parking lot, cross a street and be at work. Beautiful.

Erika was still with Billie during this period, which forced me to hold a steady job in order to keep some support money flowing into a family pot that I no longer shared.

I've always thought well of Billie for what she did. She could've made life extremely difficult for me when we parted if she had insisted that Erika go with me.

I felt a sense of urgency about retrieving my daughter, but no desperation. I knew it would only be a matter of time before domestication reared its ambivalent head in my direction again.

While biding my time I alternately partied and was alone.

The party times seemed to have occurred as a result of some kind of ethereal catalyst, breathless affairs smuggled in on a cushion of excellent marijuana and red wine.

I didn't know what I wanted to be or what I wanted to do. M. and I had grown close but not close enough to prevent her from going to Washington, for training as a something or other in Vietnam.

We had spent an extremely romantic winter together before she left, meeting in someone's home in Los Feliz. It was filled with crystalline candlelight, intimate breakfasts of mushroomed omelettes and Danish beer. M. was extraordinarily right for me but that was something I didn't clearly understand until she left for Washington.

I've had enough time to clearly think back on it and conclude that it wasn't my pride that was put in a lurch when she left, it was my state of mind, my emotions.

Stupidly, I decided to get another job. I'd heard of people having two jobs but I'd always thought that something was wrong with them.

Who was it? Brother George, I think who got me on at the U.S. Rubber Company in Santa Ana. I thought I could pull it off for a few months, make a lil' extra dough.

The way I figured was like this; work from seven a.m. to two thirty p.m. at the rubber factory—drive home to the courthouse job—four to twelve thirty p.m. It *seemed* possible. Scars

Cars. I had some kind of car that I'd purchased from a lil' ole Jewish lady off of Pico. Me, not knowing anything about the workings of machinery, dogged the poor thing to death. The only real care I gave it was water in the radiator. And the radiator leaked.

Santa Ana to L.A., L.A. to Santa Ana. There were times, after the second week, when I didn't really know whether I was coming or going.

U.S. Rubber Company, Santa Ana. Foul odor was the first thing to get used to strolling inside the place.

Foul odor, probably full of cancerous ions or something.

Insane work. People hauling wet (hot foam rubber) mattresses off of conveyor belts on their backs. Dumb jobs that some machines should've been doing.

I was put into an "entry level activity." The job involved "dancing" around in wet foam rubber discards up to my knees, shoveling these cast off bits into drying ovens.

Nothing was wasted.

George had been working there for eleven years or something like that, and he looked it. Skin was flaking from his hands, he had odd discolorations on his face and he probably had a bunch of strange shit in his guts.

Gruesome place. They had people doing things in that place that I would not have thought that one human being could've or would've asked another human being to do. Scars

Like, go into the "pit." The *pit*. Goddamn! There was this

conveyor belt setup, with something like hot tallow dripping through the slits into a basement-like deal. After a few days I was asked to clean out the "pit." I couldn't believe it. I couldn't believe any human being would ask another human being to go into that place.

Hot tallow/foam rubber drips down the back of your neck (collar never seems to cover certain spots) as you shovel this crap off of the floor, walk five steps to shake it into a wheel barrow. I felt like I was a robot with emotions.

I did it for about three days and complained at the beginning of the fourth. I don't know if it was because I complained (an unheard of number) or what, but the next thing I know I had a cushy job standing over a conveyor belt of running latex with a piece of string in my hand.

My new job was to pull the string up through this conveyor belt filled with latex to see if I saw a bubble. The principle was the same used to get air bubbles out of the clay before it is molded into shapes.

Totally insane place. They had things for people to do that were totally ridiculous. I think they were making linoleum on this conveyor belt. I didn't care.

For a while I slept on my way from Santa Ana. I have to believe that the Orisha were easing me along, there can be no other explanation. Sometimes it seemed that the whole bumper-to-bumper-twice-a-day-trip was a bad dream.

I didn't escape. I felt a little weird about myself. Why was I doing this awful shit?! I couldn't explain it to myself.

Gruesome place, the U.S. Rubber company in Santa Ana, California. Really gruesome.

After giving it some serious thought I decided to let myself get fired. Terrible place, they would fire you for being late three times. On my last day, my radiator blew, the car stalled. I was within a mile of the factory.

I was challenged. Could I get to work on time to quit? I

113

jogged a little, thumbed, got picked up by a brother who took me almost up to the gate.

I was five minutes late and I had lost my job. I was crushed with happiness.

Foul, funky space; I can close my eyes and see the stupid, stinking, lousy ass motherfucker.

Chapter 11

I think it would be awfully hard for me to ever listen to any romantic bullshit about working, not after the post office and the rubber factory.

Back to nights at the Comptom Courthouse, swabbing out the holding tank and scraping gum off of the lobby tiles, cushy job.

The custodians were a real bunch of characters, as I'm sure custodians are all over the world. We drank on the job, smoked marijuana, snorted cocaine, all kinds of shit. Memories

One night Mrs. C. came for me, took me away to my L-shaped room and, after hours of pure hedonism, returned me to the job. The supervisor of the evening, a simple soul, couldn't believe his ears when Mrs. C. simply told him, "I'm sorry I kept him away from his job but I had to have him."

Stuff like that. Somebody always had something to get

loaded on. Uppers at times, inners, outers, whatever.

M. and I were writing each other but it was almost pure bullshit on my part. I say, almost, because there was one special facet of me that was utterly real and sincere.

I wanted her but I couldn't really figure out how badly. I wrote a glorious letter every time I sat myself to pen and paper, put my feelings on hold until I got an answer and continued doing my thang.

Of all the places for it to happen, it had to be in the holding tank. I was swabbing the concrete floor with this wet, twenty pound mop, looking up at the bars of the cell door from time to time, feeling vicariously bad vibes whenever I did so.

The twenty pound mop felt like forty pounds. Swab, to the left, to the right, to the left, to the right and blimp. My back went out. I had no idea that things like that could happen before they happened.

Strange occurrence. Of course I immediately filed for Workmen's Compensation. And started going through a lot of beaurocratic changes.

It would've been a sweet scene if I had simply been trying to collect some money, but I wasn't. I was seriously hurt. And scared to death.

I was scared because I had the feeling of being unable to control what was going to happen to me. One minute everything would be fine and the next minute I'd be hunched over like a cripple.

Frustrating as hell. I didn't know what I should do.

I didn't write stories or anything like that. Letters yes, stories no.

I was placed in a Catch-22 box. I couldn't return to work without a doctor's clearance (which none of the county doctors seemed courageous enough to offer) and I couldn't get another job with a Workmen's Compensation case hanging around my neck.

And then, suddenly, unexpectedly, M. showed up looking wild and fearful. She had driven back to me from Washington, D.C.

In our letters we had reached that point, that she was going overseas or back to my little L-shaped room in Compton. She came back. I was stunned.

My back didn't suffer any improvements from the tension.

Situation: I'm trying to figure out a way to pay my bills, stick a few coins to Billie for Erika's upkeep, figure out a way to keep myself from going insane trying not to worry about my back. Different stuff.

M. took a close look at things and made a decision. We made a decision. I had asked her to come back (in one of the glorious letters), I loved her and I still do and it was going to be cool. Rough, but cool.

This is the section I've been waiting for. If I had known she existed, I would've cut off a few years and pulled her toward me sooner.

She got a job at Bob Spreen's Cadillac, in the file section. I was impressed and inspired. If I had a woman with a Masters, who spoke a couple or three languages, and was psychologically squared away, on *my* side, willing to help me by taking on a chicken-shit file clerk job, then I had to be about something. Either that, I had to get about the business of being something or otherwise I could label myself an immoral pimp and be damned.

I had no real idea what it would be but I began searching for something to do. We needed more room, ideas were demanding it.

Strange that I would feel compelled to speak about M.'s color, her race, but that's what the times demand.

I clearly saw a white woman (after all, I'd been married to one, I knew what they looked like) but beyond that. She

117

was like somebody sent from another planet, this was the person who was going to make it possible for me to write my way into life. I was enchanted by the possibility.

It's hard to say what we did for a few months, it was so strange. There I was, living in a largely Black neighborhood with a white Scotch woman who had been damned near everywhere; Bolivia, pre-Castro Cuba, American governess for a couple Swedish brats, cook for an upper class family in Geneva Savoie.

M. is a trip. She prepares some things so well that you feel a sense of occult about it.

We lived together for six (or was it seven years?) cruel, bitter, sweet, evil, mean, exciting years and we remain friends because we shared those times.

M., a natural linguist, got off into the Black language speech patter, typing stuff for me. She couldn't and didn't try to speak it but she had/has a remarkable ear and it gave her a real advantage as a typist-interpretor.

Memories   Coltrane and a move from Cocoa Street; they urban-renewed the place. Struggle and hustle. A check for almost two grand is left in the mailbox of the standing door frame of the building that had been torn down. Strange things happening.

Discovering who you are can take you on many paths; Mexico.

I had been to Mexico City with Norma, but I had never had the opportunity to experience Mexico until I went with M.

One night we threw Erika and a bunch of stuff into the Volkswagen and lit out for the sand dunes on the West Coast of Mexico.

A Volkswagen is an interesting vehicle for people to get to know the real side, you either became enemies or grow to become lovers.

From Nogales to Huatabampito is a nice ride. We lapped

it up like sweet milk.

Hot days, warm, dream starred nights, nights filled with the sounds of the Mexican countryside, Malinche screaming her innocence, Indian people.

We drove into the town of Huatabampito, circled the town's policeman standing at ease in the plaza and got directions to the ear of the town, "la oreja del pueblo."

Seeking the ear of the town almost carried us off in to the Gulf of Mexico. The "ear of the town" was going to place us on the beach, where we planned to hang out for a few days.

Late at night, I drove through a desert, you could feel the residual heat in pockets along the road. You could also see the dinner fires in adobe homes to the right and left of the road, and smell tortillas being cooked.

I don't know if it was the hypnotic atmosphere or my don't give a damn feeling but the next thing I knew we were trying to push ourselves into the Gulf of Mexico.

What happened is that the damned road, such as it was, had become a part of the beach. If we had had a bit more traction I probably would've drowned a car and the three of us.

We stepped out of the car into one of the lushest nights I've ever known. I don't know what the deal was but inside the car, there was nothing. Outside it, outside the stuffy Volkswagen, the moon suddenly full and smiling, the temperature must have been one degree warmer than our own body temperatures.

The air bombarded us with the tang of salt mixed with some kind of fragrant, flowery essence; the sand was warm, the stars sparkled. We were on the Huatabampito.

We dove into a bohemian life on the beach for three days and nights. During the day we walked the gently curving two miles of beach, casually watching the porpoises play in the Gulf (I thought they were sharks) and, one night, we slept on somebody's rooftop.

We were in a beach resort that the town's middle class used "in season." The resort consisted of ten adobe buildings with thatched roofs, a couple with corrugated cardboard.

We had arrived in the middle of the "non-season" and had the whole place to ourselves. Well, just about.

There were the squatters who owned the dog that could root crabs out of the sand with his nose, the lovely guitar player, the town crook.

The town crook was a real dickhead.

He came up to me the second day we were there, rapped a bit, next thing I know he's asking if I'd like to trip to the shrimp boats that lay to in the bay.

"Si!" we all hopped onto the idea. Interesting sideshow for our trip to Huatabampito, a trip to the shrimp boats that held huge baskets of light on cranes fore and aft to attract the shrimps.

We were cutting through the buttery waves before it clearly dawned on me what we were doing, and where we were.

Here we were, a nice looking African-American male, his Anglo-American "wife," also good looking (in a swimming suit yet) and this little bombshell bosomed/bodied Afro-Gringa ... on our way to visit some fishermen who hadn't been close to anything that smelled like a woman in three months.

Close up, the romantic ships with their spidery nettings turned out to be old tin tubs manned by men who looked like the fiercest Mexican pirates ever.

They were glad to see us. They would've been glad to see anybody, especially any female, but not in an ugly leering way.

Beautiful men, I'll remember them until the day I die. They fed us, an incredible Mexican bouillebase of turtle meat, conch, red snapper ("Huachinango"), bell peppers, garlic, olives and who cares what else. It was unreal.

The most piratical looking of the sailors brought out their

personal treasures to show the ladies—odd shaped pearls, sea horses, while I sprawled out on the deck and smoked strong Mexican cigarettes with a trio of literary types.

On our way over the side we asked them what they'd like to be sent when we got back to the United States; we were, after all, "rich Americans."

If I had been stuck on a shrimp boat for three months, I think I would've been tempted to ask for something real juicy, like a thirty year old virgin with outstanding looks. But no, not these gentlemen, they wanted something to read, pocketbooks (not nasties, just plain pocketbooks).

And we sent them, loads of them as soon as we got back to Los Angeles. I think they picked them up in Mazatlan the following month.

We did a lot of that kind of thing, even while I was working in the Stauffer Chemical factory, a place at least sixteen times more deadly than the Rubber factory.

There was a solid reason for me enduring the chemical factory; I was waiting to get a job as a community relations trainee in the Concentrated Employment Program, a real cushy situation. More about that good thing later.

Meantime, the Stauffer Chemical factory, filled with red-rednecks, super patriotic Mexicans, Gros Ventre Indians and just plain ol' prejudiced white folks. Real, real weird place.

Scars, memories . . .

'Round the clock shifts, like it was impossible to really get any sleep. Just as I was beginning to re-shuffle my metabolism around to sleeping from eight in the morning to three in the afternoon, the shift would change and I'd be on the four to twelve midnight shift. And on and on. It was as close to organized torture as I've ever been exposed to, or victimized by.

The factory in South Gate might've been something of a self-realization course for me, a Ph.D setup if there ever was one.

The factory. We were dealing with something called tripoly-phosphate and some other stuff. It looked likel granular salt when it was dry and was like slushy snow when wet. And the lightest bag of it weighed fifty pounds.

The place was run as brutally as most factories were run at the time—1968-69. And the work was beastly hard.

I did everything there was to be done in the place. I loaded pallets with hundred pound bags of tripolyphosphate. I popped a few Benzedrines, trying to stay alive on the twelve to seven shift, goofed up the modular ltransfer of a few thousand pounds of something or other and one night; feeling stupid and mali-cious, I drove a forklift through a low storage-warehouse door, with the forklift on high. The damage was spectacular.

The investigation that followed was like something out of the "Caine Mutiny Trial." Of course they never found the guilty party because they were too dumb to figure that I would do something like that.

I always had the feeling that I was going to be killed by some-body or something.

Racial goodwill was nil. We were there to make a paycheck and that was that, except for the fact that animosities surfaced anyway. The whites didn't like the Blacks, (we were outnum-bered on each shift by fifty to one) the Mexicans didn't like the whites and thought the Blacks were slightly loco. Or may-be it was only yours truly that they thought that way about. And management and labor and all the rest of the capitalistic madness prevailed.

I was working/waiting for a 'phone call from a counselor at the Concentrated Employment Program (sweet sister, Mrs. Pat Falls) and hiding out behind twenty tons of one hundred pound tripolyphosphate sacks to scribble poems.

One afternoon, deep into a search for the right word, I looked up and discovered that half of the twenty tons was about to cave in on me. I left a beautiful poem behind me.

The call came out of the blue one day, just in time. I was planning to quit. I had been injured on the job, I had had a brick dropped onto my safety helmet, I had almost been trapped in a rotating kiln, I had almost lost my mind one night on top of a four story silo as the wind pushed my body to the edge and I was becoming obsessed by the idea of becoming a writer.

Chapter 12

Pat Falls, bless her soul, had found a place for me as a community service trainee. One of the hippest jobs ever developed in the wake of the Watts Outrage. There were thirteen of us and we were like members of different tribal groups.

The community service trainees were extensions of the professional staff. The idea behind the Concentrated Employment Program was to find jobs for people who needed jobs. The trainees' job was to relate to the community, which wasn't very difficult at all.

It was a dream deal for me. It was the first time I'd ever been in an office atmosphere. I began to write a novel.

Watts, post outrage, was in a heavy state of fermentation. Everybody was a poet, a philosopher, an artist or simply something exotic. Even people who weren't any of those things thought they were.

The white power structure, (I can just see white men piled

up like bricks) feeling guilty (for a change) and scared, were pouring money into the area to try to head 'em off at the pass.

Some busy body made a study and determined that there were about four hundred aid programs in business in the area. Fo' hundred!

Lots of bullshit was happening. It seemed that the only thing you had to do was grab a storefront, invent a slogan, slap a sociological reason for existing on your proposal and hold your hand out.

Needless to say, there were many serious abuses of slogans, sociological reasons and what all. But none of it was as immoral and cynical as the hands passing out the goodies.

It was quite easy to predict that the hands passing out the goodies would only do so for just so long and, after they had ample testimony that people untrained to handle millions couldn't handle it, they could point all the fingers on their vicious hands and say, "see, we told you those (them) people didn't know their asses from a hole in the wall." Or whatever. Coldblooded white racism.

In any case it was going well for me. I had retrieved Erika from Billie, we had moved from Laurel Street to Cocoa Street and my aching back was almost back to normal.

Hard to really figure out where everything was, despite the more ordered structure of my life. What I'm trying to deal with is how the writer in me was being shaped.

I knew that some beautiful people were helping me. Jim Bradley, my immediate supervisor, and a frustrated poet, often allowed me to make use of my time in any way I felt would be most productive.

Mr. Kane, the executive director of the office I was *supposed* to be working in, peeked over my shoulder, at my embryo novel so often he could almost make a critique. At times he did.

I still find it hard to believe that there were so many people

126

in one place who were so supportive. It was as though all of the post office years before that, that were filled with nasty, mean people and uncreative circumstances had been replaced.

I was making the writer's workshop scene, in addition to John Bloch's in Watts, Louise Meriwether at Occye Slaughters' home and Mrs. Peavy's home. Publishing my own book of poems ("Me and them") turned the whole deal around for me.

M. helped do a lot of that, she and her friend, Carlyn. M. was a strange catalyst for my writing life. Strange, I think, that she should be one of the people I could point to.

She formed a contradiction for me that was psychologically uncomfortable, for a time. I couldn't really figure it out.

Here was this dyno-woman, helping the hell out of me by creating the kind of environment that I needed, and there was all the rest of her people opposing what I was trying to do. It was an up and down kind of struggle.

We tripped out a lot. And always had a mellow time. One morning (was it before *that* trip or another one?) we loaded Erika into the Volkswagen and swooped down to Guadalajara. And we ran up and down the coast like fools, from here to San Francisco in a minute.

Something was always about to happen. It happened at a party.

Sitting on a bar stool, watching the ladies send their bodies into orbit, trying to unburden my lascivious urges on somebody.

She was almost in my face before I realized she wasn't sitting down, she was dancing in front of me, tall sister, about five eleven.

She was chocolate black, beautiful, intelligent, proud and lascivious too. Some diablo-type intuition made me lean over, as she performed the popular boody-rattle of the day and whisper in her ear, "I bet you'd rather be off fuckin' somewhere, wouldn't you?"

It was as though I had touched her freak button. She paused, gave me a quick, shrewd stare through her black horn rims and flitted to another sector of the dance floor.

Half an hour later we were sitting on the side of the bed in the hosts' bedroom, sucking on tongues and trading phone numbers. It was, as the song once said, the beginning of somsthing grand.

Memories . . .

All of a sudden a whole bunch of goodies began to trot my way . . .

I'm at MGM Studios, sleeping my ass off on a sofa in my office. I'm supposed to be doing a re-write of a script that Gordon Parks, the famous, excellent photographer wrote, an adaptation from a book called *Eagle in the Air* by a woman named Robinson.

Yeahhh, I'm sleeping my ass off on the job, a dream job paying five hundred bucks a week. Sidney Beckerman is the producer, the dude paying me and I'm the dreamer. Memories in the Dreams

Memories . . .

Bud Billiken Day, August, when Dr. Martin Luther King, Jr. Boulevard was called South Parkway. Brilliant Black faces, bodies, clothes, (I'll skip the evolution of racial designations; we've always been Black/African and they've always been white) the whole thang.

It's like I'm floating over the miles of the marching Elks, ladies of the big Baptist churches wearing white gloves, young people in military outfits doing drill team movements that would bend any military academy out of shape. Balloons, color, African-American perfumes, comfort in each other's warmth. Drums coming! Drums coming! Girls with big, beautiful, black cocoa-shiny thighs and softly curving bottoms, wearing tall white hats with white tassels, ice cream bars, peanuts, red soda pop, popsicles, watermelon by the slice.

I soaked it in, the parade, and landed behind the people piled up at the curb. I saw US from the rear, all of the various shapes, sizes and attitudes that my tribe is. I checked out the silhouettes, the proud, stuck out chins and lips, the gorgeous bodies, the colors of the poeple and the music they created.

At six or seven, definitely by the time I was eight, I had fallen in love with US and shortly thereafter, when I discovered painting with a pencil, we got married, forever. Or until my death does us apart.

Yeahhh, the Southside was luxuriantly beautiful for me. I used to walk from 51st Street (on the east side of the street) to 39th Street and back (on the west side of the street) just looking and feeling. No one ever had to convince me that we were beautiful, I knew it.

There was a sense of something happening for me as I walked. I still don't know what it was. Maybe it had something to do with having the intoxication come from within.

I was intoxicated by the stones, bricks, the dazzling arrangements that took your heart and eyes from one house to the next, from one porch to the next.

The heavy smells that people from Louisiana, Georgia, Alabama, Arkansas, Haiti, Mississippi, Brazil, Texas, the Indies, and all of those other Pan-Afrikan places had bought with them.

I was in love with my people and I was one of them; what could be better?

Bar-B-Que smoke was always in the air, especially on Friday and Saturday night. The craziness of spirit that grabbed my mind and heart gave me a glimpse of what my future was going to be.

Walking up and down those lush streets formed a spiritual

connection to what my people, my tribe, was about, on many different levels. I knew, without anybody telling me, that we come from somewhere else, a more glorious place, spiritually. I knew it.

Despite the fact that I lived, everyone around me lived in the bricks that I liked, they had somehow done something with the inside of those bricks that didn't fit what the bricks were supposed to represent.

The smells, emotions and notions of the people living up and down South Parkway rushed out at me as I strolled past. I usually carried a stick during my odysseys, something to rattle on the corrugated teeth of someone's fence, my own marimbas.

Smells, O Papa Legba! smells, almost any kind of smell but cilantro, and maybe I smelled that too and didn't recognize it. The emotional outpouring was equally rich.

People making all kinds of Black love. Fights with fists, knives, dishes, chairs, whatever. Coldblooded, intellectual arguments, music.

Music   Memories   Music

Everybody loved music and played it, either live or mechanically. Real music, stuff with substance and depth. Wes Montgomery without surplus string sections, Lady Day without tracks in her voice, Deep Song, the Blues, Afro-Caribbean, Pan-Afrikan.

I've heard, passing, voices that were so clear and piercing that they seemed to be explorations of other places, Zen voices, the Gospel according to St. Blackness.

The rooms that these voices spilled from were so loaded with misery and pain that it would be hard to believe that anyone could create anything, let alone anything beautiful, under the circumstances.

But it happened and it's still happening. Music wasn't something you listened to, something you used as a background, (although that was done too) music was another facet of life.

Music was the air, the soul and spirit of whatever was happening. The wintertime forced most of the music indoors but it always surged back out in the Spring, at the soonest possible time.

Strangely, the analogy of a winter-white, forcing music into a bag, the white hairs of your head, the connection with tears and sperm shooting into endlessness, seems to approximate what has happened today. I'm happy that I heard a whole bunch of music before it was snowed under.

Afrikan things, I guess, the music, our attitude toward it (old men used to dance) dancing, our movements.

The four seasons on Chicago's Southside were incredible. I really feel that we paid no attention to winter. O yes, I know we did, but not really; if we had it would've wiped out the other three seasons.

How could you really pay any attention to a kind of numbness that grabbed your ass from September to April? I/we froze in it, threw snowballs, slid in it and, somehow, loved it a bit.

Example: What were we doing in Washington Park on a freezing winter evening foolin' around? We used to do that a lot, our little group. Donald, Benny Boy   yes, here they come, I can see their weirdly shaped lips, eyes, mouths, warped heads and bodies, incredibly tough little dudes mostly, but here and there, a big one like Mickey, the one who had me write his high school autobiography, or something like that, when I was in grammar school.

"Awww g'on, man, you can do it."

Mickey was an extremely intelligent, offensive tackle for Phillips High School, one of the best in the city. A pro, in other words.

We were different and now, whenever we run into each other, wherever, we recognize our sense of difference by being

131

unable to relate to what we shared. Some of us have tried, and it seems phony. Daisy Mae became Daisee and the children are scared to hear about what their parents went through. Or the parents are ashamed to tell them.

How to explain enjoying the winter without warm clothes, good shoes, and/or homes without heat of any kind?

But we did enjoy the winter. We enjoyed it in a way that was different from summer, it's opposite. But we enjoyed it anyway.

The first heavy snowfall (that must've made adults shake their heads in misery) called us out to throw snowballs at each other, roll up huge balls for snowmen, gloveless sometimes, play! play! play! in the snow.

Why were we in Washington Park? Why was I clutching at the thin ice around the hole I was in? Why were the people around the hole looking so disturbed?

The ice kept crackling and breaking as I made swimming movements with my bare hands and kept kicking beneath the icy hole I was in. I was too scared to surrender to a hole in the ice. What would I tell my mother, who was goin' to whup my ass good for gettin' drowned.

I'm sure that supernatural thud of a heavenly ass kicking helped me fight my way to firmer ice and pull myself out of the hole, which stretched in back of me for about five yards.

My clothes were caking up on my body but I was alive, running as fast as the ice chunks forming on my lower body would allow; I was alive.

I was going to be warm as soon as I got home. I was going to have to tell a helluva lie to cover my frozen clothes, my mother had sharp eyes, but I was alive. I had saved myself and I felt good. Winter.

If winter was a crazy time, spring drove me crazy.

Chapter 13

For me, spring was the beginning of another beginning. But then, I was always all over again. My mother and father were a beginning for me, in the sense that they always seemed new. Maybe it was because they were there and yet not there.

My mother, Lillian Trice (Hawkins), was sixteen when I was born. I'm certain that her sixteen back in 1937 was an incredibly younger sixteen than sixteen would be these days.

My father, Odie Sr., was seventeen or eighteen.

Oddly, I place them on pedestals in the back of my mind, two young people primping to go out, the air around them fragrant with dreams. Momma loved perfumes and men and Daddy loved colognes and women. They always smelled lovely to me. My father's armpits especially.

Beautiful people, my mother and father were; she a four feet eleven inch Kalahari woman and my father a cool West African brother, it was like watching two cultures meet. My mother, from the dry Arkansas and Daddy from lush Miss'ssippi.

Tempestuous, dynamic, superstitious, religious, always involved with something, in love with life.

If it didn't exist, momma would invent it. I think she may have invented my father.

Statesville Penitentiary is where I first saw my father, actually. Staring across a barrier I recognized his beauty, and what he had to endure for being Black and beautiful too soon.

And Louise, my sister. What confused lives we had. One day we might be living in the basement on 51st Street, the next day, on the westside, in the basement at 1150 Washburne with my Aunt Mary and a half dozen cousins and the next week on the northside with my uncle Eddie, in another basement.

Odd things happened in these basements. One sunny afternoon (this happened on the northside) I happened to jump from the third or fourth step of the stairway leading down to the entrance way of our place and landed on a big rat's back.

A fantastic quirk of timing had him running from underneath the steps as I jumped. I crushed his rear legs. He gave a terrible screech and dragged himself into a hole somewhere. I just stood there feeling nauseated.

Rats. Rats everywhere. In the basements they outnumbered us by the hundreds and they knew it.

I lost my thumbnail in the basement, thought it would never grow back, a two by four smashed it.

A lady who lived on the second floor took her son and me to see *The Jungle Book*. I think Sabu howling through a fake Indian jungle in pursuit of Sheer Khan, the malevolent tiger, may have been my introduction to the world of Story.

And in this basement, with all of us sleeping together, I got my first dose of clap. Very strange feeling to be seven or eight years old and have the urine burn as it drips out.

I didn't receive any treatment for it and it gradually disappeared. I guess my body went to war for itself. And won.

Kindergarten/Mrs. Bournes/the school on 50th Street on the southside. She took me home with her, fed me chicken, gravy on rice and lemonade. We sat on a back porch in a nice neighborhood somewhere and talked. She felt pity and love for me, I could feel it.

My mother, Aunt Marnie, Aunt Bessie, Uncle Thomas, Cousin Claude, his current woman, my sister too, was flattered that my school teacher would take me home. I was a bit surprised too. Why me?

And Jenner on the northside. And then Smyth on the westside. And back to the southside to Oakland School, for a few days. We moved faster than the rent could be collected.

My sister and I were being taken care of by a teenaged girl from downstairs. My mother had left me with a lady everybody called Miss Sweet.

Sweet Memories

50th and State Street, right across from Du Sable High School. Miss Sweet was doing day work at the time, which is how our teenager eased into the scene.

My reasoning about how the situation came about is drawn from the logic that a teenage girl would have. He can't get me pregnant.

My sister was playing in the other room or taking a nap or something when the girl pulled off her panties.

I can still see the fur suddenly erupt from beyond the pink of her panties.

Memories

She gently pulled my pants off, laid down on a bed (we must've been in Miss Sweet's room) and gently placed me on top of her. She whispered, as she jabbed my little hard on into her, "don't tell anybody about this, okay?"

I'm sure I must've agreed.

135

I had more than a vague notion of what we were doing. I remember her hand, the cut she seemed to be placing me in, the grizzled feeling from the fur and a certain, unmistakable pleasure from being nestled against her breasts, feeling the warmth inside her body.

I've often dreamt about that girl, about that scene, that day. We did that a few more times but it was never the same, never as exciting as the first time.

Sex. It was everywhere.

Loretta and I lived in the same building on 51st Street, went to the same grammar school and one afternoon, tripped down into the basement storage area, where there were some old mattresses. We didn't "play house" or "Doctor" or any of that. We had sexual intercourse.

I couldn't vouch for an orgasm on either side but we definitely put a lot of energy into our act. Funny, when I think back to it, two eight year old lovers.

Southside, westside, northside. We would've lived on the eastside too, I guess, if Chicago had one. We came as close as possible, a couple times, living on Lake Park Avenue, just a ripple from the lake.

I'm leery of trying to deal with how poor we were, my mother, my sister and I. Daddy is a murky figure at this stage.

I hesitate to deal with the poverty-stricken angle of our lives because of the many draggy stories the hyped up tragic-woe-woe-tales of people who talk about how hard life was on the farm. Or wherever.

For long stretches we had nothing. We were Gypsies, the three of us. My mother would often stash us with a relative, a friend or a sympathetic soul   and be gone.

I know now that she was trying to rake, scrape, steal, hustle, borrow or do whatever, to get us something to eat, to have clothes and a place to live.

We starved a lot. I was too young and unaware to realize

that the society we existed on the fringes of had programmed our starvation.

Because my mother lived each day as though it were the End, didn't seriously consider tomorrow at all, budget-wise, we were often faced with a blank page for a menu the day after a fried chicken feast.

When I say "society programmed our starvation," I absolve my mother from the errors she made. The society that starved her, educationally, psychiatrically, spiritually, simply programmed her head to pass along the goodies.

Memories, scars

I tripped back and forth to so many places in the city before I was ten years that they seem like blurs before my memory's eyes.

Periodically, since I guess it was expected of me, I'd point to the northwest corner of Racine and Washburne and announce, "that's where I was born."

Oddly, I've always associated the westside with my father's dark-skinned relatives and the southside with my mother's lighter skinned people. My sister and I, the new generation, represent a sweetly tanned compromise.

Speaking of different sides of town   the westside was a tribal reserve. We could have been a longranged branch of any of a number of African tribes.

The people on Washburne, Hastings, and street after street in each direction were African-Americans. The old Jewish landlady upstairs for whom I was a shabbas goy for a time, was the only white face I ever saw on a regular basis. The other white faces, the bloodsuckers, slithered through, making their collections for worthless insurance policies, furniture that was stapled together, stuff like that.

The Jews fringed this African section (which was never called that) in a section called Jewtown. Jewtown is a fond memory-thought for me. The center of this Jewish world was at Maxwell and the street that intersected it. Never could recall the name of that street.

A walk through Jewtown was like tripping through a linguistic circus. It didn't matter what they were saying, they were just there. And exotically interesting.

We had a helluva symbiotic number going on, the Jews from wherever they came from, and us Black folks. We went to the steelmills, the stockyards and to the thousands of shoeshine stands that were galled "gigs" or "slaves," made the money, bought it to Jewtown and exchanged it for something we thought we needed.

Years later, (I'm still sleeping my ass off on this sofa at MGM) running into the sons and daughters of these Jewish peddlers and hustlers, in Hollywood; I had to pause for a secret smile, thinking of how little the number changes shape.

I had no real understanding of the meaning of Judaism. All I recognized was that there were some people called Jews who used to rip us off a lot. To be fair about the setup though, we felt that if their love of money was great enough to make them stand in front of a wooden table piled up with stuff, hollering 'n screaming all day, in the summer heat or on a sub zero evening, then they deserved the money. That was the African in us speaking.

The Gypsies lived at the eastern fringe of Jewtown. Now they really fascinated me. From time to time, especially in the summer, I'd stroll up one side of the street and down the other side, listening to them and staring at them.

There were authentic Gypsies, dressed in long satiny dresses, with strands of gold coin around their necks, flashy head scarves, talking to each other in voices that were so beautifully deep and ragged

I heard the very best flamenco spoken, long before I heard it sung. They flowed in and out of the scene, Gypsy like.

Across Roosevent Road, the Italians had it locked up. It

was always unsafe to walk through their area.

In another direction, Poles, Czechs, Lithuanians, Letts, Estonians, people like that. And in another direction, Mexicans.

The Puerto Ricans and the other islanders hadn't really gotten the middle western part of the country in focus.

I went everywhere. If I was feeling ambitious I would pull a little wagon I had over to the South Water Market and pick up stuff from the ground. Lots of us did it. South Water was where the trucks loaded vegetables and stuff to be delivered to the markets.

A sharp eye could spot unblemished tomatoes, cabbages with just the outer leaves soiled, corn in season. Food.

The rats were, as usual, a problem. Some of them would actually put up a fight for their share. I saw some that must've weighed ten pounds. Looking at the pictures of a muskrat, a beaver, a squirrel, and a few other like types always makes me think: rats!

I was a weird little boy in that basement on Washburne/1150 West Washburne. It was, to me, that I was entrenched on the scene and, at the same time, out to lunch.

I liked to be alone and that was weird, for a group of people who took pleasure in being bunched up together. A week at 1150 West Washburne was like this in the spring of 1944-45. Monday morning. Since my Aunt Mary is a country woman we all have to get up early. She doesn't think too much of people lying in bed unless they're sick or crippled. Her word is the closest thing to law operating in our basement. Another basement. This one was a classic.

You walk down the front steps, into what looks like an air raid shelter. The steps to the first floor crosses over the top. To the left is the coal storage bin, where coal for the winter is stored, and Aunt Mary's dogs.

Aunt Mary was something like a one woman animal shelter. From time to time, she might have as many as fifteen dogs (after the latest puppies) in the coal bin.

I used to spend many hours in the coal bin, reading whatever I could get my hands on, using the shaft of light that came through a half dollar sized hole in the manhole cover covering the coal bin opening.

Memories in the dream

Sprawled back on a half ton of coal, I'd stare up through the hole and fantasize. Or I'd just sit without moving for a long time, until the dogs had forgotten I was there, and observe them. I find myself using the more scientific sounding word, "observe," rather than watch, because that is exactly what I did, I "observed."

Dukes, my favorite, a smallish, jet black dog that people used to call a fice, ruled the coal-bin-kennel. His bite, or the promise of one, was law. It was somewhat like living in a closed space with a bunch of nearly neurotic wolves. People thought I was crazy because I preferred the company of dogs to people. No telling what they think these days.

My Aunt Mary righteously disliked me for my connecting to the kingdom she'd set up. What it boiled down to is that I could get next to; I had the time to get next to the animals she owned. They loved me. I was one of them. She owned all of us.

I used to sprawl up on a pile of coal, under this little opening in the manhole and read. I still don't know how I learned how to read, but I did. It may have had something to do with the stories that my uncles used to tell as we sat around the pot bellied stove. Helluva bunch 'o storytellers.

In another frame of reference, I read the weirdest shit you could find, walking through the alleys of the westside. It pains the fuck out of me sometimes, in a beautiful way, to think that I learned, figured out, studied a bunch of garbage, to become intellectually intelligent. Funny, to me, to check out the latest National Geographic Garbageology Studies. I'd like to stack my "university" degree against the requirements of any American "university."

Uhhh huh . . . in the spring the walls underneath the street would sweat and a primeval kind of dankness oozed out. I almost found myself liking it, at least it was a change from the usual smell of dog shit.

I think I was made much keener by spending so much time with the dogs. From watching the males with their penis tips glowing all the time, I became unwired one day (hey! who is the Human Dick up in here!?) and pulled mine out to look at it. If the truth of the matter be righteously told, I was into a bit of subconscious competition with Dukes.

Dukes, immediately sensing where I was coming from, leaped over and tried to snatch a bite on my dick. (Can't you see the headline now: Dog bites boy's dick off at the tip.) I dodged his snap on my prick, pushed myself back into my pants and never tried it again. Damn! what if he had been an orangutan?

I've never been able to figure out why I did that. Maybe I was jealous of Dukes' way with the females. Or perhaps it had something to do with my doggy nature.

In any case, it was really weird, having a dog put your ass back in gear. I'll never forget Dukes. He was one of the most decisive animals I've ever been privileged to know. What would've happened if he had given me a real go at the Shepherd-St. Bernard-Setter-Poodle bitch, the one who was always blinking at everything?

On the other side of the basement, like going into a baseball dugout, we lived. I was of the people in the house but not one of them. They knew they had a nut case on their hands and it left them slightly bewildered. My Aunt Mary, accustomed to run-of-the-mill subservience, disliked my attitude so badly that she would sometimes give me the feet of the Sunday chicken, the one I had slaughtered.

I think I was the first truly strong man she had ever met and she felt obligated to break me. She didn't beat me, she was too good an animal psychologist to do that. No, her methods were more subtle. She gave me the job of making the fire in our pot bellied stove every morning. And in Chicago, on a ten degree below zero day, a basement floor can feel like the ice below ice.

The lady punished me psychologically because she had no way of understanding where I was comin' from. Our culture had been hurt so critically in certain areas that Aunt Mary (all the Aunt Marys) acted as mental drill sergeants; she was teaching spiritual survival before it became popular.

Many of her techniques have just become common knowledge ... humiliation, humble bugging-ego-crushing shit, the kind of coldblooded stuff that would prepare you for a harder life than any of them had ever experienced. She was righteously avant garde.

Interesting woman, from all points of view.

She kept the chickens in the pantry because she liked to have live food on the premises.

I believe Aunt Mary was an Iyalosa, the way she used to blend good and evil, sweet and sour, hot and cold.

She allowed us to love each other, us children   physically. Suzie had given me the clap over on the northside, during one section of time when my sister and I stayed with Uncle Eddie. We hadn't realized that my inability to piss freely was related to what we were doing. Talk about ignorance. Suzie wasn't a "fast girl." I think it was more a matter of wanting to be loved than anything else. Shit! we all wanted to be loved. None of the adults had any time for that foolishness. They were sturdy, enterprising peasants from Miss'ssippi who wanted to make certain that we had enough to eat, no matter how eccentrically we acted.

I feel that they allowed us to love each other because they

didn't have the time to be soft, life was too fucking hard.

I used to look at my Aunt Mary, Uncle Percy, Uncle Eddie, if he was currently living with us, with his super suave self, and the cousins, including Moochie, as though they were films. Other people sometimes spent the night, huddled behind the pot bellied stove. Dudes like Crippled Sam, with his withered legs and bamboo colored crutches; had three sons and kept a pocket full of money. Incredibly intelligent man who looked like a middle-aged Joe Louis. I always felt that he was a priest of some kind.

Lots of what went on down in that basement often struck me as being very African, very "In." People prayed a lot. And they took things seriously. This was before Television.

The only dramas, comedies, or whatever we had were each other.

My cousin "Tweet" was a case in point. "Tweet" had, through operations for something or other, accumulated a bunch of large scar-welts-tissue-lesions-keloids on his left eye, and a trail around the right side of his neck.

Brother conked his hair, smoked as much dope as he could get hold of, drank a dazzling amount of wine, wore a bandage-patch over an eye he could see out of (he felt it was ugly) and went around with the collar of his shirt turned up. Beautiful dude. He would give you anything he had. And loved women. And they loved him back.

This one good eye (the other one had a white cloud in it, but he could see) he had staring out at you was so warm, so lustrous with desire and courage; if I had been a girl I would've tried to lay a piece on him too.

We were tight partners for awhile, when I lived on the westside. Everybody but him thought I was a nut.

If I wasn't in the coal shed with the dogs or doing a thousand other odd things, I'd be chopping wood for winter.

"Y'all know what Odie doin'?"

"Yeahhh, I seen him. Out there in the back choppin' wood."

"In the middle of the summer. That boy is somethin' else."

I don't know, it seems that some of us were being motivated by different stuff. I was afraid of being as cold as we had been the winter before. There was something about the last winter my senses recorded   heyyyy, don't get caught in that kind of bind again.

So, I sometimes strolled around, snatching the planks off of other peoples' fences. I was a very bad/good little boy.

The southside was where my mother's people lived. Aunt Mamie, Aunt Bessie, heavy sisters, weights.

They were like figures on each side of a Ghanaian gold scale, or a Nigerian one.

I was always being transferred from one side or the other, except for the time when we went off to ourselves (Momma, Louise and me).

I was so confused, I developed migraine headaches.

Chapter 14

My mother took us where she went, and she went everywhere, on foot.

From time to time, lacking car fare, we would stroll from
one side of town to another, buying an ice cream cone or
something, en route.

Even after she got fat we walked. She didn't walk fast or
have any precise way of moving. She sort of shuffled along,
but she was persistent.

Being a nomad in a city like Chicago can be annoying.
People throw your stuff out on the sidewalk in the middle
of the winter. Cold-blooded shit.

Basements. Bowen Avenue. This basement had once been
the storage area for the building. There had been a fire a few
weeks before we moved in, the smoky wood smell stayed with
us for as long as we lived down there.

Achieving some kind of record for stability, we stayed put

for about a couple years. The Bowen Avenue "apartment" was a terrible place to live. Terrible.

You popped down through a hole at the side of the lobby, stumbled down a winding, wooden staircase, underground life. A dim light glowed at the bottom of the steps, casting shadows of people doing things in the community kitchen. We could've been Black Neanderthals.

The "community" kitchen had once been a laundry room, the big aluminum kitchen tubs at the east wall were former rinse tubs, the fractured concrete underneath was slimy with dampness, bugs and disease.

The toilet, a clapboard affair that looked like a very bad representation of a tree house, with wide cracks between the slats (we all peeked in at each other on the stool, at one time or another, to see if it was vacant) that never seemed to be free of a gruesome sewerage-disposal-plant smell, was on the immediate right.

Some "mysterious" people lived in the first "apartment" on the left side. Mysterious was the word for them because their apartment was reinforced with plywood and their front entrance was a cement exit to the street. I'm certain they paid extra for their status.

Number two, us; three, four and five faced nothing. Well, not exactly nothing. At the rear of the cubicle was a stoned up wall and, since the wall was like a dam for the dirt packed behind it and above it, it leaked.

It leaked trickles of stinky water, centipedes, ants, water bugs, rats, funky smells and, from time to time, after a light rain, fat worms.

The opposite side of the cubicle was where the door was, which faced the community kitchen. We may as well have been living in a series of turned over boxes, open side up.

The place could fuck you all the way up. I had migraine headaches the whole while we lived there. Call it sensitivity or whatever but the place made me sick.

The thought of it makes me sick, even now. But the people living in the basement were a beautiful experience.

Memories, Scars

The Whitehead family from deepest Miss'ssippi, deepest Al'bama, or deepest somewhere (wherever they were from had to be the deepest) lived in number three.

After Mrs. Whitehead, the Matriarch-Elder of the Clan, you could count until you ran out of fingers 'n toes . . . and still not come to the end of the Whiteheads. And when you thought you had run out, somebody else would show up with a lil' cardboard suitcase, a length of rope holding a bunch of clothes in. We grooved. They dug me and I dug them. Real soulful people who had a serious understanding of life.

They were country people, filled with pig sty dreams and no one had prepared them for inner-city slums.

A kind of listless, anemic, yellowed out woman who was always pregnant, always trying to lift steaming tin tubs of wash water off the old four burner (two worked) and was always having miscarriages, lived in number four. A man came to stay with her shortly after each miscarriage and soon after he left, she'd be showing again. We were like stationary refugees and everybody around played on us.

It wasn't all the time bad. The black market, meaning the dope fiends who slept in our kitchen in the winter, offered us dibs on what they stole. And they stole everything. My mother once bought me a rainbow collection of sports shirts for about ten dollars.

Jean and her son Kenny, in the last cubicle. Jean was small, very shapely, looked like a chocolate version of Cecile Aubrey, a French actress who was last seen pouting at Tyrone Power in a period flick called *The Black Rose*.

Jean was close to my heart. I don't know why, maybe it was because she was so pitiful.

She and my mother were always plotting against my assumed virginity but it never came off. I just couldn't force myself to make the midnight creep through the kitchen and tap on her door.

Henry was the main reason why I couldn't do it. Henry wasn't Jean's fo' real ol' man. He was a sadist who liked to get drunk and come down into the basement for a torture session.

The man would've been recognized anywhere as a psychopath.

The open space in the middle of the basement belonged to everybody.

It's hard to figure out how my mother, Mrs. Whitehead, her daughters and granddaughters old enough to cook, the anemic woman and Jean got together on their cooking schedules.

One solution was to put on a common pot, which was done fairly often. Neckbones, white potatoes and corn bread. "Soul" food for real. We shared.

The open space served other purposes as well. In the wintertime, the neighborhood dope fiends would creep down on us. They crept down and drooped around on chairs, milk crates and whatever, our friends, the neighborhood dope fiends.

We had a gentleman's agreement. There would be minor lapses, from time to time, arguments over the proper division of the heroin, but mostly everything was cool.

Fred Lee, Fisher, Bam 'n Baby June, Sister McMullan, Blackie, Rookie, Blue and whoever else might be a part of their pack for the evening. Like I said before, they gave us dibs on everything they stole.

I always seemed to be the one who caught somebody fixing, because I liked to get up late at night and burn roaches

(I curl myself into an even greater fetal knot on this MGM

148

sofa, feeling vaguely threatened by the subconscious memory of how gruesome life used to be. Damn! would any of them ever believe that I was sleeping on an MGM sofa, in my own office?)

I developed a weird kick, burning roaches. It was my payback for all the times I'd found them in my grits, in my oatmeal, in my greens, running out of my pants in school, crawling on everything.

I would pop out of our room about one or two in the morning with a twisted cone of paper burning and slowly wipe it back and forth underneath the bottom rank of the huge cluster of roaches papering the wall above the kitchen sink. Or above the bath tub.

I could usually fry a few hundred before they realized what was happening. Stupid, to think back to it, that I should have been trying to burn down a whole wall of roaches. I should've been trying to catch rats, but I was afraid of them.

The basement was heavy. On some weekends so many different things had happened down there, when I got ready to go to school on Monday I'd have migraines on both sides of my head, if that's possible.

Henry had beaten Jean's face into a raw welt. She had sneaked up behind him a half hour later and stabbed him in the shoulder with a butcher knife. Blood everywhere.

Jean and my mother get into a fight later on because they both dig a gambling-pimp named Red. One of Mrs. Whitehead's granddaughters had been bitten by a rat that's acting more aggressive than usual. The five pounder with the stub tail.

Frankie, the aunt of a buddy of mine has been found on the "back porch" (an open cellar at a level with the cobble stoned alley behind it) on an old sofa, drunk on cheap wine, her lower limbs and skirt stiff from the semen that's been left all over her body by the men who've fucked her through her stupor. Rape? She might've done the same thing, cold sober.

Somebody wakes her up. How long had she been out there? Days?

"Hey, Frankie, they fuckin' you, girl. You better get yourself together."

The anemic woman has a messy miscarriage all over the middle of the kitchen. Who told her to boil and try to lift fifty pounds of boiled clothes? Dumb. Dumb. Dumb.

A few days later, the slime still visible on the concrete floor, her man drops by. The anemic woman was sad to watch. She loved suffering.

Mrs. Whitehead cooked buffalo fish on Sunday afternoon and gave me two pieces.

My head pounded like someone was standing on the left side of my forehead with a hammer and chisel. I couldn't see straight and no one knew what to do with me.

When all I needed was a few hours sleep (is that why I'm sleeping on my MGM sofa?) and a lil' peace and quiet, they'd bug me by making just as much noise as usual, asking me at the same time how I felt.

I'm certain that I had at least two nervous breakdowns without anybody knowing about it, not even me.

I knew something was wrong. The place was too much.

I made it my business to check it out once, going through to New York. The building had been torn down and replaced by a building with no basement at all.

On a bright fall day I stood on the street in front of where the basement had been and cried. I felt as though a really soulful part of my past had been closed. I know how Jews who survived the camps feel.

I could never go back through those doors again.

The secretary just peeped through the door to see if I was still sleeping. They've never seen a Black screenwriter at work before. I hadn't seen one either. I didn't know how to act and I was tired. I snoozed on.

The Almo Hotel seemed to signal our final move from basements. We lived on the second floor, in the rear, with the fire escape back porch. And then to two rooms on the third floor, south side of the building. And from there to another room. Or was it the other way around?

The Almo, as it was called, was a four story brick at 3800 Lake Park. I imagine, once upon a time, it had been a good looking establishment. By the time we got to it, it had seen better days.

The whores and pimps "owned" the first floor. It was called the transient floor. They used the fourth floor as an R and R area (Rest and recreation, for the uniniated).

The other two floors were inhabited by the normal collection of people who couldn't afford to do better, felt more comfortable about being with people who drank too much cheap wine, or just simply wound up in the Almo through force of circumstances.

A few of the people could've been called the dregs, and the place was as wild as any place else and I could remember us living in, but it was not the pits. My bilateral migraines became less frequent.

"The culture of poverty," a sociologist once called it, referring to the perpetually poor of Mexico City. We were in the same bag.

Most of the elements were still present that went into the making of a horrible lifestyle; the dope fiends, the hostilities between people, the lack of common cornforts, but there was something else happening. I can't place a focus on what that something else was, it's permanently blurred. I do know that I was forming the plans for my eventual escape from all the madness.

I was a sophomore in high school and had come across an interesting book that explained why rats, jumbled together in a cage, will try to eat each other. A Something Else sense warned me that I would be eaten too, if I remained in the cage. I had to escape.

We lived in the Almo, on and off, for three years. During the off times, something that happened when Momma didn't pay the rent for a longish time, we moved away somewhere for a couple weeks, and then back again. It was as though the slumlord had completely forgotten about the previous defection.

The son of a bitch was making so much money off of these cubicles, he could easily write off a few thou every week. And Momma thought she was getting away with something.

She was getting away with a lil' something. During one of our sojourns in the Almo she sold wine. Wine is what the name was, but the stuff in the bottle was something else. It was extremely sweet and about as strong as bottled alcohol could get.

Due to some weirdass law, liquor stores didn't open 'til twelve noon on Sunday. This meant, for people who were into a case of the heavy shakes, that they would be damned near out of their trees before eleven in the morning.

Momma took up the slack. Her stock was white and dark port, at fifty cents a bottle. She charged sixty cents a bottle and seldom cleared a profit.

But that really wasn't what it was about for her, the profit motive. She wanted to help people, and this was her way of going about it.

If she had been up late the night before, playing cards or shootin' dice (she had a passion for gambling) then I'd be the one to crack the door open and ask, "red or white?"

The credit brigade wiped out any serious attempts to really create a profit margin. I could stand at the door, behind the burglar chain, and say, "no," because the wine didn't mean anything to me.

I was tasting a lil' bit on the sly, out in the streets, and smoking a lil' too, but it didn't mean to me what it meant to them.

I could see a dude at the door, trembling with the wine-want, fifty cents short, which meant only one thing, they didn't have enough to cop. Talk about cold-blooded mother-fuckers   me.

The dedicated winos realized, early on, that I was a lunatic they didn't care to deal with, me and my weird notions about no credit 'n shit.

Inevitably, the slickest ones would create a lil' commotion if they were short, say, by a dime.

"Awwww c'mon, youngblood, Lil' Bit (my mother's nickname) know me, she know I'm good for it."

Stupidly, I'd try to counter his/her argument with a simplistic one of my own.

"Wine cost sixty cents a pint."

"Awwww c'mon now youngblood, you know me, I be comin' through here all the time."

But they knew, if they egged matters along a bit, Momma would call out from the cot in the kitchen, where she was *supposed* to be sleeping, "go on, let 'im have it."

It would irk the shit out of me because I realized that our profit, such as it might've been, was blown. My mother saw it in another light.

"Look, fool," she'd explain to me, "these are our friends and if we want to get a favor, we have to give a favor."

I could see where she was coming from but it still pissed me off.

Scars   Maybe America was rubbing off on me.

One morning, the liquor store at least ten minutes away, and not open yet, one of the elderly ladies knocked for her pint. She must've been sixty at least.

Viciously, I sensed a way to get something I wanted, for something she wanted. America *was* rubbing off on me. My

153

mother was asleep on the sofa behind the transaction.

I held the bottle of wine out to her and mouth-mimed an indication that I wanted to have sex with her. I would never be able to duplicate the gestures, or the emotional fires that lit the scene up.

She looked slightly surprised, but not shocked. What the hell was there to be shocked about anymore, in the Almo Hotel?

She took the bottle in her trembling hands and waltzed to her room at the end of the hallway, beckoning me to follow. I shook my business head and gritted my teeth   damn. She hadn't paid.

I sneaked into her room just as she was finishing a hurried swab job between her stringy legs with a greasy dish cloth.

"C'mon, I'm clean," she kept saying, and collapsed on the swaybacked bed, terribly excited at the idea of doing it to a fifteen year old boy. I was out of my mind, nothing mattered, I wanted to experience everything.

Her limbs were stringy as leather cord and her womb was as dry as a buzzard's beak.

I couldn't vouch for it but I honestly believe the old lady had a climax. I definitely did. And that was it. I fled back to our room to sell more wine.

Stuff like that used to happen periodically. While preserving a goodie goodie image I frequently did a whole bunch of stuff.

I've stared at myself in the mirror, in recent days, trying to read out the genetic quirk, or whatever, it might be called, that something that offered me a clear view of the scene.

This odd clarity, in the middle of a murky situation, told me, number one, don't shoot dope even though I was fascinated by the junkies. Number two, don't drink too much of the cheap wine. With a couple partners I would stand up in the alleys and hallways, slugging my share. But I didn't drink. A modest swallow was enough to get me high, after that I didn't want anymore.

Terrible tasting shit. Some of my friends, who couldn't stop at a swallow or two, or a bottle or two, are still drinking whatever the current popular brand is.

I missed several of the "pleasure giving substances," like marijuana, for example, because I was afraid of being hooked, I saw what dope did to people.

I took a hit on the joint as it went around but I didn't hold much smoke in. I cheated, they thought I didn't know how to smoke.

I felt detached from the scene. I was always inside the circle, circling it at the same time. This peculiarity was evident to the people around me. As a result, I received respect from older people; winos, dope peddlers, 'hos, pimps, the community. And I returned it.

I wanted to shoot some dope so bad at one point it wasn't even funny. It just seemed to be such a hip thing to do. People seemed so peaceful, so cool when they fixed and nodded off.

I came close. I made a buy from the local dope fiend, went into the toilet on the third floor and snorted the stuff up my nose. I broke into a cold sweat as I got this rush through my system, like I was about to come. About to come. About to come. I freaked. O my God! I'm a dope fiend! One of the zombies that sit around noddin' all the time. A heroin addict is an incredible experience to observe.

I didn't want to have a habit that would pen me up. No cigarettes, heroin, wine or thoughtless emotional relationships.

Because high school was a definite place, the first institution I was in for longer than a few months, I often use it as a book. From 1952 to 1956 I was a student at Du Sable High School. I was a bunch of other things too but mainly I was a student.

Three layers of things stand out in my mind about that period. Aside from the heavy atmosphere in the Almo, and the heavy atmosphere at school, I used to sometimes walk to school, from 38th and Lake Park to 50th and State Street is a long walk. Or I would cash pop bottles for carfare. I felt anything would be better than spending the day at home.

I had a job, the third heavy layer. Through the aid of a buddy on the northside, who pretended that he had been Toulouse Latreced by a truck, earning him pity and a nice donation-collection from the other employees of Carnegie Drugstore, I had a job.

At first it was every other day. My friend, Johnny Fox, alternated with me. Or sometimes we would work three or four days in a row, alternate it that way. The white folks didn't care, all they wanted was a body to serve them.

I went from the hell of what home tended to be, to the hell of what high school can be for the average African-American adolescent, to Carnegie Drugs, in the Drake Hotel. Talk about going from one world to another. From the Almo Hotel on Lake Park to the Drake Hotel on Lake Shore Drive was a leap through the weirdest space ever thought of.

1953, the near northside; meaning homes with teak wood beams in ceilings that looked like auditoriums, even the kitchens.

I think it dawned on me then, these motherfuckers are rich and that's why we're poor.

I saw it and understood it. I haven't had to alter that simplistic reasoning very much over the years.

Incredible contradictions sometimes left me staggering back to my hole in the ghetto, trying to put some kind of order to what I had experienced that day.

Lady says, "I understand your people, my Daddy always had colored people around when I was growing up." And other, even more awful shit than that. I actually hated white people for a while, and I'm not certain that I've eased past the feeling.

156

Specifically, as a group, I learned that they were not to be trusted and had no consciences. No one taught me that directly, I learned the hard way.

I also discovered that individuals do exist and you must evaluate them with some kind of objectivity. Generally, insofar as the group is concerned, they should be sent back into their caves until they learn how to behave like human beings. Memories   within the dream on the MGM sofa

Carnegie Drugs was one of several shops on the ground level in the Drake Hotel.

My job was mainly to deliver prescriptions, from four to nine, not too bad. And when there were no drugs to deliver to the northside's hypochondriacs, I cleaned mirrors on the soda fountain, just around the corner in the coffee shop section. And stacked this and stocked that, all the bullshit that one does in a situation like that.

I stole a lot, food mostly. And whatever else I thought they wouldn't miss. Used to cop pounds of condoms.

Despite the racism, it wasn't the very worst place in the world to work. I made a game out of it. But more than anything else I studied the people.

Hilda, a short, middle-aged blonde devil with a crooked tooth in top front, hated me with a sincere passion.

She said to me one day, pissed beyond the fringe, "What what the hell do you think you are, a white boy?!"

I had no answer for her but I knew what she meant. It didn't matter. None of them mattered. So far as I was concerned they could kiss my Black ass.

I was young, felt strong and realized that they were both pale and weak. The only thing they had that I didn't have was money. And I was determined not to take any shit off of anybody.

The situation placed us in a neat pocket. If you wanted to act like a man (even a young man) there were at least fifty

157

piss poor examples scurrying around. Two of them will always stay in my mind, a dude named Van, and a little snuff colored, baldheaded old gent who looked like Mr. Magoo.

Van worked in the drugstore, complete with a white bolero jacket. No one knew what he really did, what his job was. Maybe he was being paid to act like a nigger, possibly.

Mr. Magoo slaved in the men's washroom. They were slime in my eyes.

They were like this; Van was one of those weird Uncle Tom Negroes who had given everything up, his self respect; his dignity. In 1953, in Chicago, (up South, but damn!, still not down South either) Van was doing a Tom act that would've put any ole time house nigger to utter shame. I used to look at him, bowin' 'n scrapin', scratching his head 'n mumblin', "yassuh, Miss Julie" and, "no suh, Master Henry" (he actually said Master!) and I felt like killing him.

I hated him with a cold, cruel passion that made him want to vomit every time he looked at me. I hated him and loved him because I understood him. He couldn't help himself, he had become a white man's man.

Mr. Magoo, the bathroom attendant was a few cuts below Van. He used to get down on his hands and knees, in the men's room, to blow his hot lil' breath on some white man's shoes and give them a last little lick with his tongue before they tipped him. Some of the Southerners used to have erections at the sight of him doing this stuff. He was a freakout, for himself and them.

The first time I stumbled onto the scene, I just stood in the door, transfixed by a sight that was really obscene. I found out when the lil' ole rascal took his half hour lunch break (the only time he left the men's room for longer than fifteen minutes) and started stealing from him.

I stole with dignity. I shined all the shoes possible during the twenty minutes he was absent. I pretended to be the toilet attendant and I did it with class.

Based on the tips I made in a half hour I could easily see that the money was there, but he didn't have to crawl around on his hands and knees to make it.

The world was opening up to me, and not because I was getting a superduper academic education. Du Sable High School, in 1953, was probably one of the worse high schools in the city.

Individual teachers were guerrillas with vital programs. They were Black, their names were Mrs. Margaret G. Burroughs, Mrs. Akeley, Mr. Moseley, Mrs. Pace and a few others. The white teachers, as a group, were prejudiced, bigoted, patronizing.

An English teacher named Miss Cleary had us write an essay, or composition, they called it. After reading mine, she accused me of copying from a magazine. Real dry shit like that.

Of course there were exceptions, but during my four years I was only taught by one, a dour, stiff shouldered Irishwoman who ran her class like an Army camp. I thank her. Dear Miss Gallagher.

Du Sable was a jock's school. Basketball, with "Sweet" Charlie Brown, Paxton Lumpkin, Shelley McMillan, dudes like that. And football and track, and even swimming, unheard of in most Black high schools.

The "eggheads" and there were a few, had an uphill struggle. I sat in a commercial geography class for a semester, oooohhing and aaaahhhing at films of basketball games our teacher (Mrs. McCloud) showed. If we went much beyond that, to doing serious work, I cannot honestly remember.

An all Black school in an all Black neighborhood. It was a kind of playground for me, like I had lived the whole adult number clean through, with every possible variation of bad times spicing it up, and now I was in kindergarten.

I suspect that there were people in school going through

the kinds of changes I was going through, but we were submerged by the general population, a group of twenty-five hundred who all seemed to have more than I did.

I liked football, so I played, no matter what the hardships were. I made first string in my senior year; considering the number of nineteen year old, semi-pros we had at Du Sable, it was a major league accomplishment.

I ran track too, for some peculiar reason. In one track meet in the University of Chicago fieldhouse, I found myself leading the pack by a half lap and stopped.

I could never make the coach, Mr. Hillman, an ex-walker, who walked like an ex-walker, ("you think that motherfucker is a sissy?") understood that the open space in front and around me bewildered me.

I had the same thing happen to me at football practice on a few occasions. I'd break into the clear and suddenly feel stranded, or simply out of place.

I've long since dealt with the fear of open spaces. I was in high school, doing as much as I could, but I had to avoid most of the social scenes because I didn't have the clothes or the poise to cope with what was happening.

Strange, that peculiar thing has been with me all my life. Attacks of the "shies" have often made me flee across the street or run through alleyways.

O well
Memories

Chapter 15

My work day at MGM is finally over, I can yawn myself awake and go home to work on this script.

Five hundred dollars a week, more money than I've ever earned doing anything.

These motherfuckers   they nourished my dreams and then blew cold nightmares across my pillows. But first, the dreams.

From MGM, doing a re-write, to Universal for a couple original screenplays (unproduced), to Warner Bros. for one, to Paramount.

I was hot, the money was setting into my pockets like rocks. Time to make a trip to Europe. Why Europe? I can't answer myself with "why not?" that would be cheating. No, I couldn't imagine going to Africa, home, with M., with a white woman. No, I didn't want to do anything like that. Europe, it had to be.

Memories

Loftleider Airlines (Icelandic) to Luxembourg. I'm on my
way to see what Miller, Hemingway, Wright, Himes and the
rest have been talking about. To find out how Hitler and the
white man came about. In some ways it was close to that.

I had this strange theory, this notion in my skull that made
me want to understand how the white man was forced into
being. I wanted to know if white genius and evil came from
a common spring. Or whatever the hell it was that caused
the white man to be the way he is.

Loftleider Airlines had two planes, one going to Europe
and the other coming back. It was cheap, the flights from
New York to Luxembourg, and they were gorgeous. It was
like a giant 747 party across the Atlantic.

I thought Luxembourg was the navel of Europe, filled with
Nazis. We tripped out a few minutes after we got a hotel room
and everybody I saw looked like a version of Walter Slezak,
but menacing.

We were headed for Nacka, Sweden, a suburb of Stockholm, to stay with friends of M.'s. John and Margreta. I was
on a research project.

Belgium was a looser version of Luxembourg. Holland was
a trip; the mores of Amsterdam were like: Do anything, just
don't get caught. Denmark was a tip off that I was into heavier
material than I thought.

Scandinavians, Danes. I had the impression that we were
in a place filled with a passion for material goods, but at the
same time there was a cold-blooded spirituality about them.
Especially after three aquavits.

It was 1971 and very little attention was paid to a Black
man and a white woman. In Amsterdam we wound up being
given a room *because* we were a mixed couple. It was strange.

But it wasn't the racial paradise that some of the fools who
went over to fuck white girls thought it was. You could see

that. Anybody with eyes could.

John, Margreta, four year old Nina and the baby, Thor.
Nacka, Sweden.

Memories

Cold, but very little snow. No one could figure it out; cold,
but very little snow.

Nacka was a condo setup, company executives and their
wives. I think John worked for Shell Oil. He drove a Benz
and was one of the first white men I'd ever met who understood and could explain what a white man was. John was Norwegeian and married to a Swedish woman, living in Sweden,
maybe that helped the analogy.

John, calmly, "Don't you see, my friend, when a Swede
or a Norwegeian or a German, comes to America, they are
forced to be white. They are forced to play the game."

"What do you mean?", innocent me speaking.

"Well, a whole set of circumstances have been set up to
encourage the Norwegeian, or whatever, to be "white," to
subscribe to the North American idea of what a "white" man
should be. It automatically makes every white man

"And women too," Margreta added, obviously ahead of
where John was going.

"It automatically makes every white man a racist, whether
he likes it or not."

I realized, after our third evening of this kind of logic, that
I had tripped to the wrong place. I should've stayed in North
Dakota and dug into the glassy layers of sociology, or whatever it was that created the immigrant public relations man
who decided to pick racism as a prevailing ethic. People sometimes forget that there could've been another hipper system,
set up.

In any case, I had picked up a valuable piece of info, "white
men" were not born, they were made. For some reason I felt
relieved. What would you feel like if you felt that the beast

163

was irreversible?

I began to see a different Europe after M. hurried away to be with her dying father. Suddenly I was in a white European setting by myself, no white woman from North America to relate to.

I fell in love with five or six women traveling from Stockholm to Copenhagen. It was easy. They were beautiful creatures, blonde, wild, un-American, not guilty in the first degree, at least.

In Copenhagen one evening, taking a night on the town, a Danish feminist let me know that, "You don't fool me, you are not from Mississippi. You Blacks from the 'States give me a pain in the ahs. You can only think in terms that the whites in America have instructed you, you are blind to the way much of the world sees you.

"My great-grand parents never owned slaves, I feel no guilty trip about you. I am a Danish woman and I would fuck you if I wanted to. But not because you are, or you say you are, from Mississippi."

I don't know what's happening now but in 1971 Copenhagen was the mellowest city in the world, for me.

The natives were sophisticated, far sighted and secure. They, after all, had gone through a lot of problems to remain Danish. And they had traded in human beings. But the guilt was missing. I could read it in people's faces.

I partied around the clock for a bit. Someone was always taking me somewhere.

In Sweden I understood Bergman, (Ingmar and Ingrid) in Denmark I understood the Viking mentality. Many of the Danes were authentic "white man."

In the clubs they moaned and drank bier, they nostalgized, they loved (a bit crudely, I thought) and ate a lot. But they struck me as being healthy. And besides, I've always liked fish.

From Amsterdam, I decided to hop over to England. I knew I would find something that I could add to what John had laid on me about "white men." The English; some of the best "white men" the world has ever seen have come from England.

It began to show up on the overnight ferry from Holland to Harwich, England. The Irishmen on the ferry drank black beer, sang songs and got quite "Black," some of them.

An international trade union something or other was going on. The ferry was filled with beautiful women from the Caribbean Islands, Africa and England.

Picture three gorgeous, really gorgeous, colored women, ranging from vanilla to deep cinnamon, sitting in a booth in the ship's lounge.

The lounge is loaded with African men, "Frenchmen" mostly from the sound of their voices, but a bunch of "Englishmen" too.

The Englishman exchanged peaked brow signals with me, as though to say, "Whot d'ya say, old boy, shall we 'ave a go at it, hmmm?"

The Englishman and I slipped into the booth beside the trio as though we had rehearsed it. I was charmed by the idea that I could be flirtatious with a sister from Uganda, a Barbadian sweety pie and a pre-Rasta sister from Jamaica, with an Englishman.

Having a good time with most women, even in these challenging times was a con game that only the serious undertook. Who knows? If you weren't careful, you could wind up getting married. It has happened.

The Englishman was devastating. I had never seen or listened to a white man who knew how to talk to Black women. Most of the conversations I'd ever heard, even between married couples, bordered on the absurd. Or were stiffed by a lack of gayness.

We all fell in love immediately, but it was late and we all

165

had things to do tomorrow. I wanted Frances Kulewa, the Ugandian, the way a man in the desert wants water. She felt the same way. We shook hands goodnight and steam flushed out. We was hot. The Englishman disappeared.

England. England was a bitter pill for me. I got a room in Earl's Court, went out and recklessly spent all of my money because I was going to receive a check at the American Express office the next day.

No one told me that the English Postal System had gone on strike, and carried a bunch of other systems along for the ride. Within two days I was destitute, poverty stricken. And no one knew when the strike would be over.

I had paid my rent for a week, nothing else to do but hang in there, get a toehold. I knew it was going to be rough after the following scene took place in a small English library, London branch.

I felt compelled to think, as a writer, I'm sure I'll get some kind of aid if I go to the library; after all they have books.

I eased into the place, looking for someone who'd be sensitive to a stranded African-American writer.

Shit! If I started in the far north, thinking that I had found the true white man, I knew I was wrong after England.

"Uhhh, 'scuse me, lady ... uh, Miss, I'm a stranded, well, the problem is that the postal strike, as you know, hah, hah, has prevented checks from coming through.

I can chop wood, clean, do anything to get a meal. I haven't had a decent meal in three days."

There could've been more but the look she had on me murdered any other words. She looked at me as though I were a gob of syphilitic spit. Or something.

I couldn't make myself believe that one human being could respond to another human being's plight the way she was responding. Even if she thought it was pure bullshit.

"See heah, you must help yourself now, we are no longer

166

responsible for you people, step aside."

I was confused. I didn't know if she thought of me as one of the thirteen colonies. Or a West Indian who was trying to run a game on her with a middle western accent, North American style.

"Beg pardon."

"Step aside, I say, step aside."

She calmly strolled through the stacks, pulling out books about horses and cats. I was devastated. Not so much because of her specific reaction, but the reaction she provoked in me.

I knew her, she was the pure version of the Southern white woman. England was going to be very educational.

It took a week (seven days) for John Askeland to squeeze ninety-five dollars through some kind of channel, circumnavigating damned everything. I don't know how he did it but suddenly I was affluent.

In the interim, before my affluency took hold, I had bombarded the Amerikkan Embassy with pleas for help. I mean after all, I was an American citizen, wasn't I? "Don't mean nothing," they said. Or   "really?"

In the interim, I fasted. I don't know why I had a jar of Danish caviar, a small bottle of catsup and a large Swedish chocolate bar in my ditty bag. I don't know why but I was real glad.

In order to get ready for my gray-grained, blue-ceilinged, nippy-to-the-bone London day, I would fortify myself with a kind of tomato catsup soup with caviar eggs in it, followed by a couple bites of chocolate.

My urine was as clear as spring water, my shit didn't stink and my sense of smell became acute. I was starving for fish. I didn't know I was fasting.

One day I strolled into this restaurant around the corner from me, the one with the chickens twisting around on a spit, and politely asked the big Swiss blonde at the cashier's desk to loan me a chicken.

"Do vhat? Vhot do you vant?!" she practically screamed.

I suddenly felt like I had been caught trying to steal a watermelon. Or borrow a chicken.

I squeezed the words out of the corner of my mouth, San Quentin con style, trying to calm the young lady down with that approach.

"Yes, I don't ... uhh ... have any ... uhhh, money right now, I'm expecting ..."

She wasn't deliberately trying to loud talk me, it was just her way of speaking English. I got the whole story in two days, trying to get ahold of that chicken.

"It's the custom for girls from our town to come to England, to learn English. The boys usually go to France."

I couldn't figure that out and I never got the chicken either.

Like the day before I became affluent, I bought two pieces of candy that was loaded with alcohol in a five 'n dime store. I couldn't believe how loaded I got from those two pieces of candy. No wonder English school boys looked so glassy-eyed.

With ninety-nine dollars in English pounds in my pocket I felt no appetite, at first. The Indians steered me back into the fast lane with a goat curry that tasted like fire balls of meat, with a taste of pepper. It was gon' be awright.

There was nothing to do but ease back across to Holland, and slowly make my way back to Luxembourg.

On the night ferry back to Holland, I stood at the rail watching the English lights grow dimmer. Now I had experienced the real white man (and woman). I knew something of what made English fops think they could go to sections of the world and set up their own system of whatever. They had no respect for the colored people of the world.

I came to the conclusion that they were sick, had always been sick, and would always be sick. Recent news stories about the English racial problems anoint the theories that I've carried around since my visit to dear ol' England. The Afrikaner is a super example.

Amsterdam, the second time through, really turned me on. I dug the color of the city, the colored people of the place who had a lot to do with the exotic aromas that drifted over the canals; the Indonesians, the Africans from "Dutch" Guiana, the Malaysians, the Chinese, Japanese, the Dutch, who seemed as exotic in Amsterdam as everyone else.

An evening in Brussels, a stopover. I don't know, what was I doing? Just strolling around Brussels, killing a few hours, having missed this Uganda trade unionist sister. Oh well. Anyway, just strolling around, sniffing at this smell that old Europe has. It's centuries old piss, dead men/women, blood, fresh bread, stews, a certain kind of musk and a bunch of other things.

The brother's name is Tyrone. We spot each other; you can always tell another African-American when you see one in Europe. There's something about us.

We exchange the usual bullshit, real happy to discover "home folks." It can get deep over there. It would be absolutely fascinating to find out, psychologically what happens with the Afro-American's head in Africa.

Tyrone is from Monterrey, California, a place I had never associated, being from Chicago, with Blacks. African-Americans.

Tyrone was gay, I think. But that sector of his life played only a small part in our relationship. We fell in love immediately.

He took me to this cafe and tried to speak French. He was funny, funny, funny. He was in the cast of *Hair*.

Strange, I think to myself. Here I am, in the middle of wherever it is that this place is, preparing myself to listen to a brother from Monterrey, California, sing hippie songs in French.

Surprise! whenever it came around to Tyrone he would wind up singing in English. It was all quite slick. Quite

He could sing his ass off, fortunately. I was deathly afraid, at one point, before he opened his mouth, that he might sing the way he spoke French.

We went out after the show with a Belgian friend of his named Lupu, or Lupo. Anyway he was a wolf. After ten minutes in one cafe Lupo had picked up a couple English secretaries who were trying to masquerade as French shop girls on vacation.

The night began to get different. They took me to a weird private club somewhere, place looked like a Quanset hut, huge.

The tables, or pillows, mattresses that the people lounged around on were placed on floating islands of concrete attached to the Quanset hut walls. The waitresses were all six feet or taller, the air reeked with hash smoke and marijuana and a couple Afghans played on the sandy floor, skipping over couples copulating down there.

I couldn't figure out what was going to happen between the women Lupo had picked up. I wasn't particularly attracted to either one of them. They reminded me too much of white women from back home. The semi-passive feminists.

We talked a lot of shit to each other passing the pipe around. I couldn't figure out why Lupo was silly to me, a grown man who acted like a kid. Pussy had driven him crazy.

I tried to prolong my stay in Luxembourg but it wouldn't have meant anything; like, what the hell can you do in Luxembourg?

I thought real hard about it, coming back. I understood how Hitler, Mussolini and all the rest of the tyrants had developed. I had checked out the orderliness of the Swedes, the severe approach to life. The Danes are a kick, I decided, very open to life. The Germans scared me. Just outside Hamburg, a couple policemen got on to check us out for "chocolat und zigartten!?"

I couldn't figure out why they were interested in those two items. Why not coffee and donuts? It didn't make sense to me but they were seriously on *the job*.

It was the Storm Trooper arrogance of their attitude that made me decide not to get off in Germany. A six foot three inch German policeman with icebergs for eyes is scary. I see it in the Los Angeles Police Department at times.

The trip back to the United States, wearing shoes that were too tight, (why did I buy shoes in Amsterdam?) was a head shrinking session with me and my head.

Europe? Why didn't you go to Africa? I left that alone after explaining to myself that it would not have been emotionally cool with a white woman, no matter how much I loved and respected her. And there were other reasons too.

I saw Europe as a playpen. For an African-American, it would have to be. I always heard Black people say, "we had fun in Europe." The African-Americans who went to Africa never said, "we had fun." They would say, "we had an experience."

I've heard the same thing from Japanese who've tripped to Hawaii, and then, maybe, home.

Abroad. Shit. I'd been abroad, something the average Hollywood agent expects to do, at least three times a month.

Back home, Memories   scars

Chapter 16

My big ole artist friend said, "come with me, you'll dig it." Going to San Francisco is what he wanted to do, to pick up some clothes, including a Draculan cape that someone had given him. I went for it.

We got to Frisco and he *introduced* me to this beautiful Okinawan-Japanese girl-woman; it was lack of understanding at first sight. We fell in love.

San Francisco used to be capable of falling people into love. I don't suspect that it's changed very much.

What happened?

Well

Memories, sweet memories . . . it was raining in San Francisco and we got caught in it. I don't know what it was raining but it was contagious.

The girl was nineteen, from Hawaii, of all places, with sugar cane juice oozing between her teeth and waterfalls of shimmering black waves cascading onto her hips.

Her size was Sansei and she was full of love. I had no idea what to do with her except love her. She was a complete bummer for me. She smoked too much dope, was too loose and had almost no ambition.

In addition to everything else, she was confused. Confused about her identity (many Japanese-Okinawans have a weird idea about themselves), confused about her position as a woman. Confused.

I didn't need any confusion but I knew I needed her. She wouldn't be of any use to me as a help in writing. I could sense that. She used to wear her skirts wrinkled. She was going to go from bohemian to conservative, it was written in the stars.

One dope ridden, Metaxa-sipping weekend was enough to secure the feeling that a new woman was in my life, in a new way. I was stunned. What the hell could we do together?

Driving back home, we talked about what had happened (my friend and I) and neither one of us could make much sense of the whole business. He couldn't believe that I had fallen in love with a wild young number from the islands. And I couldn't believe it either.

Back in Los Angeles, being reasonably successful for the moment (it *is* feast or famine, honey), I found my head swimming with memories of what we had done.

Bam! I shoot out of the crib after two weeks of missing her and dart due north, taking the Gorman route. The car farts itself into a breakdown and I wind up being forced to call M. for help. Damn!

It was a strangely weird time for all of us. I love M., I love J. and I love A. and maybe a couple other people.

But for now, it's J. And M. performed one of the most graceful curtseys I've ever seen. I know she was wounded but she wouldn't allow herself to bleed. She became J.'s friend,

174

and a better friend to me than she could ever be, if that's possible. We will always be friends.

J. and I gave up the struggle in August of 1983. It had become too much for both of us. She had gone from predictably bohemian to conservative. And I was still being forced to deal with a world that had/has no respect for the African-American writer's experience. And damned little feeling for themselves, if you read the movies well.

We wandered up and down, in and around, J. and I did. We lived for six weeks in a friend's apartment in the "Jungle." We lived for a few months at the end of a deadend street (Mariposa off of Santa Monica) in an apartment complex with hundreds of cats.

We moved to an apartment on Clinton and Van Ness. The ceiling was so low we could reach up and touch it, five feet six or so.

The fool upstairs made it a memorable place. And the fact that we slept on the floor.

We were struggling to stay together and to keep each other together. I got a movie script to do for American International Pictures. We were disgusted with Amerikka. We decided to flee our low ceilinged apartment, to go to Spain.

Why Spain? Who knows? They say everyone gets a wild hair from time to time.

I see us now, like idiots in a dream, struggling through snow drifts in New York with seven pieces of luggage, five of them large.

We must've looked like super bag people. Real stupid, though. Why we had to take seven pieces of luggage across the country and then think about taking it out of the country is something that I will never be able to figure out.

We pawned one of the bags in New York, or sold it. Anything to get rid of the weight. Why didn't we get held up? I don't think the stick up men could believe their eyes. Maybe they couldn't believe that we had anything of value.

New York-Luxembourg-Brussels-Paris overnight. We missed the train to Spain. Funny, the way it happened. There we were, surrounded by all of this French hustle and bustle and suddenly we slowly became aware "dat de trann done gone."

We were pissed.

However, there was nothing to do but wait for the next one. Dammit! which meant an overnight stay in the train station.

But before that I thought I would end up getting my skull cracked by the Parisian version of the Los Angeles Police Department. There we were, just sitting in one section of the train station, nodding and cursing.

These two little dudes in raincoats put in an appearance. They seem to be selling something. We don't speak French. I attempt to get rid of them so that we can nod until morning.

A young Frenchman saved the day by patiently explaining to us, to me, "dese air d'police mon."

They were simply trying to let us know that if we had missed our connection, there was a special place for us to stay.

I felt like a weirdo. That's one of the things travel can do for us, you can be made to feel like a weirdo. I think it's a healthy experience, for healthy people.

The "flics" directed us to the railway station official waiting room. Seems that a few of the natives had missed their trains too.

Overnight in Paris, why not make the best of it? We checked out the cafe across the street from the Gare d'Austerlitz. French fries and a bottle of the best French burgundy we'd ever had; us, the ones who lurked up and down the aisles of the cheap foreign wine stacks for good French burgundy.

The French looked at us in a variety of ways. Weirdos, interesting, couple, foreigners, wine and French fries? We took another bottle of the beautiful grape with us.

I think we were down to about five and a half suitcases.

I felt married to what I had to do with them. Finally, we were on the way to Spain.

We made love in Irun, on Spanish soil, between train connections. Very interesting way to get to know people on their own soil.

The train ride from Irun to Madrid was almost grotesque. At one point, we shared a railway car with a family of Portuguese peasants who looked Neanderthal. They were so backwards they thought J. was a Japanese spy. Hard to say who they thought I was.

We were traveling and I think we were happy. We grew to love certain qualities in each other. I found that my Hawaiian passion flower was tough; would bitch and complain but keep right on stepping. She grew to love the fun in me, I think.

Arrival in Madrid on the coldest dawn I'd ever experienced in my whole life. It was high plateau and cold. Cold, cold, cold.

Following our good instincts, we found a room in the Plaza Matute and settled into living in Madrid.

We liked Madrid, except for the cold. I felt it as a man's city. The feeling was strong about that there.

When we stopped for our first coffee and cognac in the morning, it was different than when I stopped alone.

It was gorgeous on some days; we pickn'ked in the park and wandered up into the Tablao Romero at three a.m. Flamenco at its purest, coming from one gypsy who had a voice like a castle. Or a Beduin tent.

But it kept getting colder and colder. We were told that it might get colder yet before it got warmer. After two months we decided to go south. Shit! why go to Spain and freeze, we could've gone to Chicago for that.

The south of Spain, sunny, warm. We settled into the city of Alicante.

Alicante will always be my metaphor for Heaven, Purgatory and Hell. At different levels it was all of that and more.

Her name was Sarafina Sanches Bou Gomez, or "Fina". And she was the dark river we had to cross over, to find the three levels of meaning. Fina had made herself our friend one evening over a few glasses of cognac.

Complicated lady, you could tell that right off. She looked a cross between an ugly, pouchy version of Irene Pappas and a Flamenco queen. I thought she was a Gypsy until I found out that she hated Gypsies. But she loved their music.

She was a member of one of the wealthiest families in town. They owned one of the two concessions on the mile length beach. In the summer season they needed crates to transport the profits to the bank. They were rich. And yet Fina worked in the public toilet underneath the concession and lived in a shotgun apartment on the fifth floor in the redlight section.

She, like the rest of the place, was filled with contradictions. It was Spain and the people were serious about themselves, but they also knew how to laugh. The laughter had many forms.

She persuaded us to come out of our high priced corner of the Residencia Nava and live with her, she would kick in some meals and we were guaranteed to have big fun.

We fell for her shit. We moved to the fifth floor of the old building situated on a cobble stone street. Our room was under a sloping roof. The wooden windows opened out onto the rear of the town, the real Spain.

Alicante became home. It had an interesting rhythm, spare, lean. No one wasted anything, bottles were re-used and clothes were sewn to last a lifetime.

Fina began to work her magic. Under the influence of her favorite wine, Tio Pepe, the worst wine made in a good wine making place, she would sing. Or do a few movements of an Asturian dance while peeing on herself. She never seemed to notice when she peed on herself, I can only surmise that the piss was like a kind of passion released.

Just when you thought you had had your total fill of her, she'd creep up with something that opened up more room.

Her son, Alberto, was a case in point. He was a certified juvenile delinquent who was as much a reflection of his crazy mother as he could possibly be.

I forgot America a little bit, in Spain. It wasn't so much that Spain was so great, it was so different.

In a few months I grew to like the rhythms; the steady, but relatively unhurried pace of Alicante.

There was a weight there, something serious about life going on, but still time to have a cognac. Fina started driving us insane with her lifestyle. She was a loser.

No matter how much money she had, she wanted to buy two day old bread. And then, hours later, while strolling the streets, buy an expensive piece of chocolate.

Spain, the best wine for pennies. And Fina craves some stuff that even an American wino would think twice about consuming.

In many ways, she was Spain. It was possible, after a while, to understand the mentality that was responsible for conquistadores who bashed Indian babies' heads against tree trunks and then baptised them, so they wouldn't go to "Hell."

The way she pardoned Alberto's cruelty to the dog, a beautiful little animal they called Curro. Alberto would try to bend the dog in half, like a piece of cotton candy. Or pull his jaws apart. Or pull his tail and try to wrap it around a stick.

The Spanish in Fina couldn't/didn't want to come to grips with our sensitivities, after all it was, "only an animal!"

In our little room facing the back of the city, the real Spain, I fell deeply in love with J. for awhile. It was cold and rainy in Alicante, but it was light years away from the pleistocene bone chilling glacial cold of Madrid.

Fina was like a thermometer. She knew when we had dinero

179

and when we didn't, and she adjusted her attitude accordingly.

When we had dinero she was hot on us; when we were broke she was too cold, too cold. I watched J. deal with her on a woman to woman basis and admired her strength.

Fina was the kind of person who made you want to embrace her or kick her ass. She was not a person you felt neutral about.

Sometimes I could see J. as the Spanish saw her and I wound up being as confused as they were. She was obviously an Asian, but what kind? And from what sector? Was she a Japanese from Japan? Or a Korean from Paris? Or Thai from New Jersey? Or what?

Honestly, I loved her most during our hardest times. It evolved to that. The day we walked across town in a chilly Mediterranean air to the post office, only to find that the motherfucking check wasn't there, it had been delivered (by our sherry loving postman) to Fina's sister. Talk about humanity in the beaurocracy.

But I also loved her during the easier times, those afternoons at the beach with wine, cheese, grapes, sausage, bread, and innocent children asking adult questions

"Are Negroes and yellow people allowed to get married in Los Estados Unidos?"

I was really impressed by her quick way with the language and the art she produced. She painted and sketched and drew beautifully moving pieces. One of the pieces was a canvas showing Jesus on the cross in the form of a stiletto. The Spanish creamed at the sight of this religious dagger piercing their hearts, drawn by a sashimi person.

But it didn't matter, none of it. The San Francisco scene, the Los Angeles-Jungle-Mariposa scene, the Spanish scene, the romance was over. She wanted a guaranteed whatchima jiit, and I wanted Freedom.

The romance romanced itself out. I think we both realized

it the minute we landed in New York, but it took about five more years for our lives to completely separate.

Upon our return to the Big P.X. (somebody once called it that) I got a job, "Odie! please get a job, dammit! help save yourself."

I got a job (through the efforts of Ralph and Vince, Mafiosi at Cedars-Sinai Hospital) as a janitor at Cedars-Sinai Hospital. It was a manna-from-Heaven job.

My hours were from four to twelve thirty p.m., only on Saturday and Sunday. I had bought the time to write by getting work.

After the first month I had figured out where they kept the gourmet food for the V.I.P. section of the hospital, meaning the filet mignons, the breasts of exquisite chickens, the lobster tails and the good wine.

It was so simple I thought I was being set up. I would punch in, swimming up stream with the rest of the fish, and slide over to the third door leading to the food lockers.

A word about the caste system. Anyone wearing the red striped short smock and carrying a trash baggie could get away with murder. I did.

With my red striped smock and a trash bag I would plunge into the filet mignon locker (they were labeled) or the lobster locker, fill up the trash bag and very, very casually stroll downstream, stash the goodies in my car trunk and dash it all home on my lunch hour.

They didn't seem to have anyone in charge of that section, or it probably changed people so often that they didn't know who was what.

One afternoon, feeling viciously greedy, I overloaded the trash bag with chicken breasts and it burst in the middle of the people swimming upstream to punch in.

They parted as though I were a rock in the middle of the river. The harshest look I got, even from a couple of the righ twinged Pilipinos was neutral.

"He's getting away with it, check that out. Why didn't we think of that?" Making two hundred beds a day for four fifty an hour doesn't breed much patriotism.

It was a matter of time before I was caught or fired. Fortunately, I got fired. If I had been caught stealing steaks they might've had me operated on, Cedars could be tough on a janitor.

I teamed up with another man for awhile, he'd push a clean-up cart next to the third door and we'd fill up his trash barrel with lobster tails. Or whatever. We got so heavily into it one night we had to make four trips out to our cars. And we felt nothing. The hospital was rich and stingy. I used to wonder sometimes; is it fair that a surgeon should get thousands to perform an operation, that would be jeopardized if the custodian hadn't scrubbed the place beforehand, and the custodian only received pennies. Who really saves lives here?

Of course, my fellow employees thought I had a mental problem. They were nice to me, though.

Jobless, I worked harder than ever. I was getting pounds of stories written while the former Bohemian ragged me. She couldn't make herself belive that I was actually going to continue to write, what with things looking as white as they were.

We were both cooled out by the Sears Radio Theatre. The Sears Radio Theatre introduced me to a bunch of fantastic actors and actresses. I learned a lot from them.

The breakthrough was happening in my media-land career, I had a chance to write what I wanted to write and get paid for it. It was the Golden Age of Radio for me, personally.

And then, of course the Depression, as inevitable as Death.

But now, here in this year, so many pieces of writing are flying off in different directions and sending checks back that it seems that all of what has gone before is paying for itself, but then, it's always been feast or famine, even in the beginning.

PART II

Read this as though you were sharing a 3rd dream with the writer.

Odie

Chapter 17

He geared the car down to first and sat on the shoulder of the road in central-New Mexico, stunned by the colors of the dawn, the crisp blues, lush purples, billowing whites, the mellow orange.

"A celestial majority," he spoke to himself, trying to invent words, a concept, for the dawn that was happening in front of him.

Driving on, minutes later, he settled back into his pre-dawn thought patterns.

The times when we made love and didn't realize that we were doing it were the best of all. How old should people be before they begin making love?

The road seemed to shimmer as the early morning sun rays glanced off of the asphalt.

So many roads, so many dreams

He smiled at the memory of his first wet dream. Cold, in

the middle of the winter time, semen gluing his hips to the sheet, a warm soft glue coating his shorts. What kind of dream had it been?

His smile broadened. A furious dream, crammed with warm bodies, steam spouting from their pores, firm flesh slipping open to welcome him, to gently suck him into the core of something so hot that he physically exploded.

He shuffled uncomfortably, trying to reposition a troublesome erection. It was all a dream, had been then and was now. It had to be. How else could he explain being alive?

He turned to stare at the horizon to his left. There was always a floor in his dreams, a place where things were prevented from dropping beneath or beyond.

The exit onto the off ramp was automatic, the gas guage was registering half.

"Filler up?"

"Yeah, filler up."

The accents were beginning to change. Back on the road, the sun in full bloom.

The blue Chinese woman. The blue Chinese woman. He stared at the cloud formation. It wasn't that the color suited her but the outline, the incline of the head, the way the hands were gracefully laced in her lap.

For most of his teenaged years she had pursued him through the streets of Chicago, from 43rd and Cottage Grove to the cold structures on Lake Shore Drive.

Utterly strange woman, ethnically; furniture store Chinese painting in a sea blue tint, the eyes and hair ink black, cranes flanking each shoulder.

Sometimes she met him as he turned foreign corners. She showed herself in Copenhagen one afternoon. He had been drinking aquavit and smoking hash all day and was feeling too exotic to tackle the possibility of disillusioning himself. He regretted his decision later.

Had she really been flesh and blood or part of his state of being high?

In the dream she inhabited with him, she was always silent. From time to time she made small, complex motions with her graceful hands, or she would smile, in a cautious, gentle way.

He felt that they had one of the strangest, and yet one of the most perfect, relationships he'd ever had with a woman.

She offered everything and promised nothing. She was his, an abnormal perception that had been reproduced thousands of times. And yet she was his, his in a way that no real woman could ever be his.

In odd corners, strange places, he knew she would be there. She was always in his dreams. Thousands of blue Chinese women and he was in love with one of them.

The cloud formation began to acquire a bluish tint.

Beer. Nothing but beer and it ain't nothing to write home about.

He poured another mouthful from the can and made a disdainful face. Why don't Americans make a really good beer?

A subtle change beginning to happen with the landscape. The ground seemed to fill up more space, the sky seemed larger. He took careful note of the fact that he had crossed the New Mexico-Texas border.

The dream was an old favorite. He had as much of everything as he needed and he was passing the rest along.

The sudden grey flash of a coyote chasing a rabbit across the narrow strip of highway didn't surprise him, he had imaged the scene the evening before, years before.

Thoughts always seemed to be rehearsals for his dreams.

The inner tube was dragging him farther out into the lake. Where in the hell was Mooney?

The tube drifted around to face the shore, allowing him a chance to estimate what his chances of surviving were. It was too much, the chances were beyond his scope, he couldn't imagine being back on shore, for a minute. But the idea of death was even less imaginable.

A half hour of frantic splashing and peddling, coupled with the idea of not being alive, saved his life.

Yes, thoughts were rehearsals for his dreams.

"You got any good beer?"

"Son, we got Pearl, it don't get no better than Pearl."

The accents had slipped completely into another sphere. It was more than solid language now, it was sound and history.

At two rest stops and one restaurant, jacking himself up with black coffee, he listened carefully for the sound of "nigger." Or "boy," at least.

Texas stretched away from him on all sides. Texas, the year was 1958 and he had just spent an unhappy two weeks in Mexico City with a neurotic wife. Texas; he had not been certain, the first time, that he had been in Mexico City. It had been an unreal experience.

Mexico City was an afternoon in a Mexican whore house talking to a blind pimp about how misunderstandings are created.

He literally felt the weight of the truck pressing on his rear bumper. Damn truckers! They act like they own the whole fucking world!

Mexico City, as ancient as the Aztecs, as modern as New York, and just as cynical.

He opened his mouth to sing after driving through Texas for a day and a half. So much Texas. Too much Texas. In the middle of a song about a woman who wouldn't do right, he quietly settled into a depressive mood.

The rat droppings beside his leg and the fierce prints on the dingy white sheet told him everything, it hadn't been a dream after all.

The sewer smell of wet fur brushing against his cheek, the

scratchy feeling between his legs, the feeling that made him clutch his genitals protectively, all of it real, none of it a dream.

And yet, he rationalized, he had dreamt it, had visualized the small, curved fangs, stared into the beady-cunning eyes and felt the damp fur.

The evening air felt moist and heavy, began to have a fragrance that he'd never been exposed to. He nodded absently as he whizzed past a sign that told him that he was in Louisiana.

Anything but more Texas, anything.

Black, driving through the mystery that makes Louisiana so distinct, produced a slight case of paranoia. Trying to escape the feeling he made a conscious decision to think about pleasurable things.

As usual, the rehearsal for what happened, his sweet-stuff-times, had been thought years before it actually happened.

The drums said it on this occasion and he was one of the players. Really balmy night on the Point in Chicago.

He straightened his back and squared his shoulders, recalling the dream.

Armando Peraza, Mongo, Julito Collazo, Carlos "Patato" Valdez and La Lupe had joined him for a bembe, a little celebration of life.

The mood was set after the opening prayers. Armando, as impulsive and energetic as ever, set the pace with the softest, smoothest guaguanco ever played. Mongo faked an exchange and took the quinto, smiling back at Armando.

Collazo and Patato built a rhythmic stage for him to climb onto and La Senora began to hum.

There was magic in the feeling his hands carried to the drums that evening.

The soft slapping of the wave quietly pulled him back to his drive through Louisiana. The drumming faded as he pulled the car over to the roadside.

A primeval darkness, lush aromas, a full moon glittering on the Lake's surface, millions of insect sounds, a world of rhythm. He got out of the car and sat on the roof to stare at the moon, the stars, and to listen to the music of the night.

Angola. He couldn't come to grips with the forces that brewed the word into his consciousness. Angola.

Angola, Louisiana, Angola, Africa. One, a symbol of degradation, the other, a symbol of freedom and glory.

Angola. He spread himself onto the roof of the car and closed his eyes, the urge to dream under a sky loaded with stars weighing him down.

He woke up an hour later, drenched in a Louisiana sweat.

He slid down from the roof of the car, conscious, for the first time, of snakes. Louisiana was where snakes were, someone had said, once upon a time.

A few careful steps away from the car he urinated on the moist, rich earth.

"Upon thee, sweet'n sour Lou'siana, I piss," he mumbled as he shot his stream.

Onward.

Midday in the middle of New Orleans found him staggering through the streets, intoxicated by the atmosphere of the streets and the beauty of the women.

For a half hour he stationed himself on a corner, or paused in the middle of one of the city's blocks, to stare at the women.

They moved past him, fleecy figures, their feet barely touching the ground. African goddesses garnished with slashes of brilliant colors. Indian ladies, their faces carved from reddish-brown stone, earth tuned.

The Creole women, not meaning those French or Spanish women who were descendants of the first generation born in the New World, but another kind of being, caused him secret thrills   of a spiritual nature and some not so spiritual.

He had no measure, no catalogued definition for the impact they made on him. They walked up to him, stared into his stare, obviously attracted to the wholesome attitude of his look, yet puzzled.

He developed an oblique method of seeing that allowed him to take them all in. Within four hours he felt as though he had been seduced in a way that no other place in the world would ever be able to seduce him again, excluding Rio de Janeiro.

Coming to the outskirts of the city yoked a sense of melancholia onto his emotions.

He sang a few wordless songs before he realized he was on his way into Mississippi.

Borracho con suenos. A book of thoughts, drunk with dreams. Dylan Thomas. Art and Black Fantasy. The best telephone conversations were the shortest. Excellent marijuana has never achieved, with the Puritan sphere of influence, the proper consideration.

Sentence associations worried at him, mocked him for fifty miles.

It didn't matter that it was 1981. What mattered was that it was Mississippi. Texas and Louisiana had only been rehearsals for the emotions that Mississippi dredged up in him.

How many lynchings? Rapes? Brutalities?

He gripped the wheel, his eyes, ears, feelings, his skin, an antennae for survival. The people at the stoplight looked at him. He stared straight ahead. They were white, meaning trouble. Odd feeling, it wasn't fear, he was too deeply in Mississippi for fear. They eased in behind him after the light, obviously to reaffirm that he was from out of state.

He glanced at them in his rearview mirror, weighing alternatives if they started bumping his car or doing something equally ridiculous. White boys could act so weird.

191

A three baton length pole with a lead center. He tried to remember where he'd picked it up. Didn't matter, he decided, that's all he had.

Alternatives. He felt his best chance for survival, if they didn't have guns, was to stop his car the minute they bumped him, grab his stick and go kamikaze on them.

Having validated his out of state status, they drew up alongside him and grinned like monkeys before they roared on into the night. He felt sudden loneliness. And the urge to cry.

Careful driving took him onto an off brand street and up into what was obviously a white residential section, it had to be because he had not crossed any tracks, any "demarcation" lines.

The night air blew in on him, grim with sea smells, magnolia, wisteria, jasmine, danger.

It would be simple. They would drive past, spot him, circle the block, block his gateway and kill him. They would be the police, a car load of beer swilling rednecks, a couple middle class vigilantes, anybody white.

For a few minutes he slowed from twenty-five to fifteen, driven by paranoia. What was the point of driving around? Wasting gas, when he didn't know where he was or where he was going?

The dumb hopelessness of the situation forced a curse out of him.

"Shit!"

He felt no confidence in his ability to explain to any would be captors why he was driving around and around this way. Since when did any white man in Mississippi listen to any Black man, and really take it seriously?

The strong fish odor and the Gulf water sloshing against the shore to his right, just beyond the wall, offered him renewed hope.

If the Gulf was to his right, all he'd have to do was turn

left onto one of the broad, magnolia lined avenues and keep a straight line into the center of town.

He made a left and drove on and on and on   until he had returned to within two blocks of where he had made his turn. Something was not working out.

His guage was registering a timid quarter tank.

"Damn! That's all I need!"

Approaching the back of the figure ahead of him pushed his consciousness into a twilight zone.

A man with a medium sized stick, something close to a deerstalker cap on, a smoking pipe, walking a large, three quarter length-tailless dog.

From the rear, passing under a dim street light, the man cast the reflection of a giant shadow.

He wanted the car to make more noise. Should he blow his horn, tap on it? No, that might not be too cool if the guy happened to be one of those I-hate-people-who-shake-me-up-types, especially Black people.

The choice was between running out of gas in a white neighborhood or running the risk of asking an uncooperative Ku Klux Klannie for directions back to the highway. To hell with it!

"Uhh, 'cuse me, buddy, could you give me directions back to the highway?"

Underneath the semi-deerstalker cap, the man's face was bronzed and crinkled with wrinkles, composed even though he was surprised.

"Lost, eh?"

"Yeah, lost. Uhh, could you   ?"

The white man's hard, crisp diction caused him to blink involuntarily. "I know, surprises a lot of people hereabouts. I'm from Vermont originally, retired down here five years ago."

He took super careful note of the directions being given.

He had only been a couple blocks off of the highway going through town. Just a matter of making one more right turn.

"Thanks a lot."

"Don't mention it, glad to help."

He concentrated on following the directional instructions given him, almost holding his breath with the effort. An on ramp and traffic flying past him as though they were carts in a giant supermarket aisle told him that he was back on the track.

New Englander. What difference did it make? He was still white. He rubbed his hand across his stomach, wishing that he had a drink or a sandwich. Something.

Gulfport, Biloxi, Pascagoula. On into deepest Alabama.

Something about the South made you say "deepest." He yawned, screamed a few times, hoping to frighten himself awake, finally surrendered to his weariness. At dawn into the back seat for a long nap, smiling at the thought of being in Momma Eva's presence again.

The midday humidity coated his face, made him feel as though his body were immersed in a thin layer of water.

Momma Eva. How many Momma Evas had he known?

At least half a dozen he decided after an hour of driving and seriously thinking on the subject. This Momma Eva, in Magazine Plateau, Alabama, was another facet of the Beautiful Black Woman he had been privileged to know in his life.

The car in his rear view mirror bothered him, it had been behind him for awhile. Rednecks out for midday fun? What?

They were too far behind to clearly see their faces. He slowed down and pulled off the road, to let them pass him.

He laughed at the sight of the greyhaired Black couple as they wheeled along, doing exactly fifty-five miles an hour.

"The South can make the brother paranoid."

He spurred himself back onto the track, being careful to stay five miles within the speed limit.

Momma Eva.

Mobile ninety miles.

He frowned, trying to recall the circumstances that had interwoven their lives.

A friend had introduced him to a lady from Magazine Plateau, Alabama, or more precisely, from Prichard, Alabama.

Over nachos and a couple pitchers of margaritas in El Cholo, she had spooled out the story of a group of people who lived in Magazine ("across the road from Prichard") and were known as the "Africans."

The "Africans," she patiently explained, were the descendants of a group of Africans who were brought to Magazine Plateau around about 1858. They were reputed to be the last known shipload of people destined for the slave's life in America.

A wave of supercuriosity forced them to investigate the situation, to trip down to Alabama for a close look at the "Africans."

Mobile eighty miles.

All of the evidence that he and his friend had been able to uncover made it plain that these folks (Momma Eva) were exactly who they seemed to be.

The ship that they had been brought over on had been beached in one of the channels near Magazine and could be seen (according to usually reliable sources) up until a few years ago.

The story had fascinating implications. If these people were descendants of the last shipment of Blacks, why weren't they known, historically?

No one cared, it seemed. Well, two persons cared. Mrs. Emma Langdon Roche wrote a book called "Historical Sketches of the South," which was as much about her white psuedo liberal 19th century attitudes as it was about the "Africans."

195

And Zora Neal Hurston, baaaddd Black lady of letters, had written an article on them, back in 1927. Beyond that, nothing. It was as if no one cared.

One of the town's better con men had bullied his way into ten grand by telling the controlling white folks a few outrageous lies. Beyond that, nothing again.

Alturism had forced him and his friend to start writing proposals, to try to get money to document the "African Experience." It was an uphill movement, all the way.

Mobile, seventy miles.

He started humming a spiritual

Momma Eva. How often does any of us have the opportunity to become friends with someone eighty eight years old?

She made them pay her two visits before she answered the door and face read them for at least five minutes before allowing them to come inside.

Inside, there was warmth, love, spicy feelings. Momma Eva was beautiful. Her daughter, a sixty some year old sweetheart, was also beautiful.

A few days later, after absorbing one of those soul food smorgasbords that had everything *but* chit'lins attached to it, they split the scene, each wondering how, in what way could money be raised more quickly to do what had to be done.

The money was still being pursued but in the interim, he was making another visit.

Mobile   sixty miles.

The song slipped and quavered to a minor chord ending. For the tenth time since he had started on his trip through the South, he asked himself, "What am I doing?"

He shook his head and smiled wistfully. The question hadn't found an answer yet. Maybe it never would.

In Magazine Plateau, Alabama, he knew he was going to talk with Momma Eva and have another helluva dinner, he knew that.

First, a few words with the lady's mother and younger brother (brother and mother of the woman who had alerted them to the fact that the Africans existed) and onward to Momma Eva.

Spun around in a weird circle, not quite lost but close to it, in the old section of Magazine, where they have "hollers."

"Uhh, 'scuse me, I wonder if one of you gentlemen could direct me to Mrs. Jones' house, Momma Eva?" Best not to try to sound real Southern.

Bunch of snuff dipping, grey grizzled old timers, hanging out on a friendly porch.

Real pregnant pause, fingers caressing grizzled chin hairs.

"Who you?"

"I'm   I'm one of her sons visiting from California."

Surreptitious comment . . . "Lookadat, car called a Honey Bee."

"Just to visit. I haven't seen her since last year."

They do a quick bit of telepathic verbalizing, several give him a hard face reading, checking for internal warts.

He had never, not until the South, felt that his face was being studied as closely and seriously as now.

A chorus of abrupt actions broke the impasse.

One man spat, another grumpled deep in his throat, another one tilted his ancient neutral shaded hat back on his head, one of them spoke.

"Keep straight 'til you come to the first openin' 'n make a right, her house is right down there, in that holler."

"Thank you, sir."

"Uh mmm."

She made certain that she knew who he was before opening the door. And then greeted him warmly, but without excessive surprise. It was as though she knew he was coming to visit her.

Before and after the chicken, rice, lima beans from the garden, the dollops of hot water corn bread, the lovely crisp salad, the home made pound cake and ice cream, they sat on the front porch in the cool of the afternoon and talked.

Mostly it was Momma Eva who talked because she had the most to talk about. At one point he had the illusion that he was a section of some off brand type of hallucinogenic picture.

Belly puffed on gourmet soulfood, mind being polished and honed by an old lady whose brain was as sharp and clear as any he had ever been instructed by.

Most of what she spoke about was transcendental. The words served her purposes but they could not be recaptured to say what she had said. No one could write her attitude down or spell out that infinite morsel that translated itself by the quick gleaming of an eye.

Ailing a bit but not complaining she allowed him to experience a glimpse of what goes thru a mind, what happens in a brain that has never been boggled by alcohol, vicious reasoning or reckless passions. A Christian Black woman who took the religion that had been hoisted onto her ancestors' backs and made it work.

"I love everybody."

"Even the white people?"

"Everybody."

She used a few familiar guideposts to illustrate points that had worldly implications.

"Mankind better be careful, this earth can't stand too much more tamperin' with."

An afternoon, a lifetime, sitting beside a person who didn't cast out evil vibes, had no mean comments to make. He luxuriated in her company, realizing that each moment meant an investment that would grant him maximum benefits for the rest of his natural life.

Later, waiting for the bridge to be lowered for his crossing

198

to the other bank, he felt the urge to turn around, to return to her porch. The urge was eased by her advice to him as he drove off.

"Go on now, there's lots more to see and do out there."

Chapter 18

There was Nashville out there.

Now why this woman started calling him is something he had never been able to explain. The calls had started about nine months before his trip. The first three or four calls dealt with questions she had about how to establish a writing workshop; after that, her many psychological problems.

He had tried to be helpful, tried to say the right things into an ear that was obviously troubled. He had tried to stop her from calling, period.

Now he was going through her home town, wondering whether or not he should get in touch with her.

The evening gradually soaked his car in darkness - his life bubble—he had nicknamed it. The sound of crickets and the zum of his vehicle lulled him into a fantasy/dream state.

What kind of person could she possibly be?

Where in the hell is Nashville?

His tires crushing through the gravel on the shoulder of the road warned him that it was time to pause, take a nap.

He climbed into the back seat, seriously considering the wild possibility that the lady in Nashville might have the key to a whole new section of his life. He dozed off, twitching into a disturbed sleep, impatient to meet this person he had been talking with for nine months.

Hours afterward, crossing the Tennessee state line, one thought pushed all others into a corner.

This is where the Klan got started.

The entrance to Nashville seemed to be a neon wall of motel signs. He made an absent-minded exit from the freeway, subliminally lured by the flashing lights.

Wonder if she lives nearby?

He nodded off between sanitized white sheets with a silly smile on his face. Imagine, a hotel room a half block from the Grand Ol' Opry. Wonder if Charley Pride is on the set?

An hour later he pushed himself out of a dull, heavy, stifling nightmare, perspiration dripping in frosted streams down his temples and forehead.

They had cornered him in a field, ten or fifteen or thirty murky creatures in robed sheets and ugly, mean looking white hats, tall and pointed, serpents tails.

They spread-eagled him on the ground, built a fire, heated poker irons in it. His screams were muffled by dirty rags stuffed into his mouth; he was in their power, helpless.

His eyes glazed from the heat of the pokers as they pulled his pants down and slowly, deliberately moved the white hot tips of the pokers toward his groin.

God. I'm glad it was only a dream.

The morning offered him the sight of wide hatted hillbilly types parading past his window, letting out an occasional ''rebel yell' as the spirit moved them. They were revvin' up for the Grand Ol' Opry.

"Yeah, I'll be right here, waiting for you."

Sunday morning, an hour to wait for the mystery woman's arrival.

He took a shower, dried himself, flopped across the bed and stared up at the ceiling.

What the hell can I say to her?

He sat up on the side of the bed, jarred by a sudden attack of nerves. What the hell am I doing here?

Energized by a series of contradictory thoughts, he quickly dressed. A cold beer?

He raced down the stairs to a liquor store a half block away and raced back with three bottles of Heineken dark.

Something to calm my nerves, he rationalized. After chugg-alugging the second bottle, he decided to shower again sweaty from his run to the liquor store.

The more he thought about it, the less he could put together about their relationship. They knew practically everything about each other, from nine months of exchanging information, but had no clear cut notion of how they felt about each other.

He saronged a towel around his waist and propped himself against the headboard, sipping the last bottle of beer. Why was she taking so long?

Maybe we're in love?

He seriously considered the possibility, swishing a mouthful of beer from side to side.

No, not love, he decided. How can you fall in love with a woman with three children and a dependent husband? Especially if you were already in love with someone else.

No, not love.

The mystery of it, he decided, slumping down on the headboard. It was the mystery of it.

Halfway through the beer he was almost surprised to feel a detached, cold-blooded erection easing up on him.

203

Ohh nooo

He shook his head and frowned. No, seduction and fornicatory activities had ever entered his mental picture, but it had now and he quickly undraped the towel from his waist to prepare for it.

Noooo   ah!

He started to get up and put his clothes back on when the first knock came. He rolled his eyes to the ceiling and implored heaven or somebody to tell him why he was even thinking about trying to seduce a neurotic woman. He knew she was definitely neurotic because he had put in nine months as her pseudo-shrink.

She had three children that she was absolutely neutral about, she didn't really love her husband and she wasn't terribly fond of herself. She dropped valiums by the dozen, was black, African-beautiful and as fucked up as they come. A schoolteacher, of all things.

"Ahhem! Come on in, it's unlocked."

Several more urgent knocks followed.

"I said come on in, it's unlocked."

She swept in obliquely, all large lustrous brown eyes and coltish legs. The minute he saw her he knew he was in for a bad time.

She was Black on the outside and a tortured white on the inside. Her daddy had been on of the town's imminent types; not in Nashville, but in another, smaller town, and she and her three sisters were illegitimate. And everybody knew it and they (the sisters) were extremely sensitive about it.

Completely wired up sister. Had watched enough soaps to last a couple lifetimes and was trying to create her own.

"I really wanna write, that's what I really really wanna do, write."

She was warped.

"I told my husband I was comin' to see you."

"You did what?! I mean, why would you   why would he have to know that you were coming to see me?!"

Subconsciously he almost threw the covers off, to hurry and get dressed. He could imagine the headlines: "Visitor to Nashville is shot in motel by irate husband. Another black mess."

She read his impulse. "Awww, you don't have to get dressed. I just meant that I had thought about telling him."

He felt vulnerable, naked in more ways than he cared to feel. Why would she play around like this?

He felt trapped underneath the covers watching her pace around, concepts, words, notions, ideas spilling out of her in gushes.

Any lustful urges he might have entertained were completely destroyed by her neurotic behavior. A schoolteacher?! God! the poor children.

"May I have a glass of water?"

Her sudden request, in the middle of a rambling, hard times type story, caught him off balance.

"Uhhh   "

"Thank you much, I'll help myself."

He watched her as she dashed to the bathroom, placed one-two-three pills far back in her throat, turn on the faucet in the bathroom sink, cup her hands and guzzle a couple handfuls of water.

None of their conversations had prepared him for this . . . this experience. He wanted to ask her what the pills were, uppers or downers? but decided not to. He'd just wait for the action and pray.

They were uppers. If she had been operating at one hundred miles per hour prior, she had increased her speed by one hundred percent. He stared at her. Attractive woman, strong traces of Indian blood within the Black mold; high cheekbones, long legs fitted into fashionable jeans, see-

205

through blouse, trendy hair do. Neurotic. Neurotic back in the sixties, the types who were always saying, "I don't know where my head is, like, I mean, I've got to find out where my head is."

"I don't know where my head is, really."

"What?!"

"I saaaid, if you were listening closely, I don't know where my head is."

He laced his hands behind his head and studied the lady. You could almost feel sorry for her.

I wonder what happened in her life to put her in this state?

Listening to her he used all of his psychic powers to try to push her out of the door. What was it you were supposed to think, in order to make things happen?

It wasn't necessary to utilize the full whammy, she was going anyway.

"I have to go do a few things, pack a few clothes and I'll be right back. We can leave then."

Unable to conceal his amazement, he stared at her.

We can leave then. What did that mean?

"What do you mean by   we can leave?"

"You're taking me away from this awful place."

"I am?"

"Uh huh, yes."

There was no argument he could make, he knew that. She had made up her mind.

"You will be here when I get back, won't you?"

He felt the impulse to tell the truth, but discretion and the survival instinct told him to lie.

"Yes, I'll be here."

A weird lucidity flickered out at him. She knew he was telling a lie.

"You promise? Cross your heart and hope to die?"

He followed her eyes to the car keys on the dresser. Oh

my Gawd! if she takes my car keys I'm in real trouble.

"I promise."

"Cross your heart and hope to die?"

"Cross my heart and hope to die."

She still didn't believe him completely but her attention was diverted by the sight of him making the sign of the cross above his heart.

"It shouldn't take me too long, I'll be travelin' light."

She paced around in a circle for a few moments, completely taken over by the chemicals gleaming in her guts.

He wanted to close his eyes and blot her out. But that was not to be. She was there, talking about going home to pack.

"Uhh, how long did you say it would take you to pack?"

"Not long."

She suddenly stopped pacing and plopped down on the edge of the bed.

"You look older than your voice sounded."

He forced himself to try to put what she was talking about together, to give it a focus.

"Older?"

"Well, you know."

Abruptly she popped off the side of the bed, opened the door and posed, a silly-vicious grin on her face.

"Should I leave it open?"

"Nahh, I think you better close it."

She stepped back inside and closed the door behind her.

"Oooops! I'm not coming in, I'm going out."

Real ditzy lady, doesn't know whether she's coming or going. Poor baby.

She eyed his keys again and made a subconscious feint toward them, grabbed control of herself, opened the door again and was off. "Be back in a half hour."

His body untightened, his mouth formed for a long, drawn out whistle. Dazed, he hopped out of bed and hurriedly began dumping his clothes back into his suitcases.

Sweat trickled from his armpits, beaded on his forehead.

Gotta get outta here! Gotta get outta here before she comes back!

The desk clerk, a long limbed, laconic, good ole boy, couldn't quite come to grips with the situation.

"But y'all paid up 'til tomorra noon."

"Doesn't matter, just give me the key deposit and

"Cain't make no refunds."

"I don't want a refund."

He snatched the two dollar key refund, raced to his car, fumbled his way out of the motel exit in the wrong gear and forced himself not to look in his rearview mirror as he sped out of Nashville.

"We can leave then

The words echoed past the throb of his motor. Poor woman.

Oh well, he rationalized, you win some 'n lose some.

Next stop, Chicago   "Baby, when you see me comin' won't you raise your window high?"

Chapter 19

Typically, despite the fact that it was late April, the trail leading to Chicago began to frost over the minute he got on it.

As usual he wheeled into the city limits after midnight.

"Wonder why I'm always driving into this city after midnight?"

He thought back to the times he had flown into the city. Those times had inevitably occurred during the daylight hours.

The heater of his car waged an uphill battle against the shafts of chill that penetrated his bubble.

"Chicago," he mumbled and brushed an icy tear from the corner of his right eye.

A cold ass walk to school thru hip high snow, so young and healthy as to be unreal, unaware of what the deal was. Too ignorant to be afraid.

He came off of the expressway at Stoney Island, popped

into the first telephone booth he came to. Good spot, a liquor store close by.

"Well," the sweet-voiced lady of his friend said, "You can always stay here."

Beautiful, a place to stay, complete with loving friends.

He popped into the liquor store for a half pint of Chivas Regal, something to help him do battle with the cold.

He made an automatic left turn, west on 63rd Street, suddenly homesick for familiar scenes.

Driving between the metal pillars of the "El," feeling lonely and a little drunk, he laughed aloud, passing remembered happenings.

The corner where he had stood one summer afternoon, just watching, cataloging, studying and attempting to understand People. The corner near where he lived, on Kimbark Avenue, where he first lived with his first wife, a malevolent bitch, if ever there was one.

In the streets. He drove slowly, picturing moments, fighting the urge to park and stroll.

"That wouldn't be too cool," he reminded himself of the realities of strolling around Chicago after midnight, circa 1986.

He made an impulsive right turn at King Drive and sped north to 43rd Street. He paused on the green light, undecided as to whether he wanted to drive down 43rd Street (East) toward the lake, past a sector of his childhood, or what.

After a few blocks the tears started. By the time he reached Cottage Grove, he felt as though he had been savagely beaten about the head with a lead pipe.

"Damn! I'm glad that's over."

He sucked the corner out of the bottle and threw it out onto the grass beside the expressway entrance.

The Outer Drive, shadows and lights glancing off the lake dried his tears, dulled some of the home grown ache.

He had always loved the lake, even when ice covered the pharoainic rocks bordering it.

He glanced to his left, hoping to see the outline of the Almo Hotel on 39th Street. So many nights spent restlessly awake, listening for the sounds of what was; the brawling, the cussing, the turmoil. Lots, lots of mostly bad times.

The lights on the expressway were lit by halos around them, gorgeous, irridescent patterns of memories. 31st Street, what was her name, the girl with the rosy cheeks and the black rimmed glasses?

Buckingham Fountain, the downtown lights, a life style time flickering past him. Never knew what downtown was all about until I graduated from high school; just another Black-in-the-hood type. His mind shot back west to "Jewtown," (even the Jews called it that, f' Christ's sake!) to the sounds of Oriental wailing sessions, to the weird sound of Polish, Lithuanian, Estonian, Russian and Yiddish. On Black ears, huh?

And the westside was *black*, blacker than some African villages. The people were Black, the streets were Black, the houses were yes lawdy lawdy! Black, the politics were Black and the situation was Black. But most of them didn't know that. Sometimes the people weren't exactly Black or any other color, really.

Sometimes they became pure Human. But everything else stayed the same. Cold-bloodedly.

The Drake Hotel frowned down on him. They had hated him at the Drake and he had hated them back, in spades.

"What the hell do you think you are, a white boy?!"

"Naww, I think I'm a Black boy."

Drug deliveries to skanky looking old white women who would leave their purses, with the money sticking out, where he could see it, and sometimes rip it off.

Lush white women, girls actually, who draped themselves in sticky apricot guaze to answer the delivery boy's ring-ring-

ring, or so he fantasized.

Homosexuals with Afro-Cuban record collections. The Drake Hotel kitchen, where the chefs operated. It flashed through his consciousness as though it were on a screen.

Afternoons on Oak Street Beach, Copacabana, Puerto Vallarta, Mazatlan, Acapulco   feeling sweet and proud in a skin that they were roasting themselves to acquire. Black has always been beautiful.

Down Lake Shore Drive north. He sucked in the night air, the lake breezes, the feeling of having survived cooling him out.

Colored people never lived this far north when he was growing up, or else he couldn't recall whether they had or not. The far north side seemed so cold. It was even cold to look at. The houses were cold. Majestic, but cold and forbidding.

"School days, school days, dear old golden rule days . . ." The sound of his voice startled him. The music was by Dizzie Gillespie.

School days in schools on the westside. Smyth school could've been the role model for the Blackboard Jungle. Oakenwald, Fuller, Forrestville, Oakland, (for 1 day), Jenner on the northside, a few others, all serious training centers for the ghetto life, not too much education happening.

The scenes flashing thru his mind, of people being crushed, caused him to grind his teeth together.

The teachers: "You know what you are, you are just dumb."
"Don't pay any attention to her, she's black *and* ugly."
"Why can't you people speak correctly?!"
"I don't know why I'm wasting my time with you people . . ."
The hammer blows of segregated Chicago, of racist Chicago.

He topped a rise and stared at the translucency of the lake for a minute. Old friends, he and the lake.

Chicago nightmares and orgasms, lakeside nights with brittle endings, lovers, would be lovers, may have been lovers, should be lovers, nights in the joints, talking deep shit to featherweights.

Dingy rooms, clean but dingy. Artificial flowers sprouting in ceramic holders beside pale, hollow cheeked pictures of a Nordic Jesus, an odor that could better be described as more of an atmosphere than a smell.

Years of accumulated perfumes, heavy incense, roach sprays, human musk, harsh soaps, chit'lins, greens, Black folks from Miss'ssippi, Arkansas, places like that.

Sometimes a lucky seven day candle flickering over in a corner, all kinds of vibes, feelings, spiritual notions flitting in through the door, the windows, bubbling underneath the linoleum in the kitchen and front room.

The second floor, within ear rattling scope of the "El" trains clattering past the back door. Almost habituated to the noise, the people within the dingy rooms go about their business.

No music comes from the ancient radio, no current news is discussed, no one seems to care who the next president will be or what the last one promised to do.

Outside, sirens constantly scream, people in serious trouble walk the streets moaning.

The cold, sleet, hail, snow and ice are mean companions for these African transplants from Little Rock and Greenville.

Some of us walk slowly through the winter, usually at night, listening to the crackle of the bare, ice whipped trees. Some of us study the gossamer cobwebs of the icicles leaping and glistening around the haloed fires of the dim street lights.

Aunt Bessie and Aunt Mamie stare through the one hundred and sixty years of their veils at the snows making water for another turbulent spring.

In their dreams flowers curl up and bloom on the fringes of this terrible street, colors brighter than the sun wander around inside their dreams, stabbing them with shards of hope.

A week later and it was all over, he had done the usual Chicago thing, had stayed up 'til all hours, done the endless drinking that was supposed to indicate that a good time was being had, had held the lovers, the would be lovers, may have been lovers, spent nights in the joints, talking deep shit to featherweights.

Chicago had become a drag, he decided, one thousand miles west of the city. There was a time when a visit was something to relish, a time to reaffirm good memories, trip thru friendships that had endured. No longer. The place he visited now was a violent, coldblooded, cruel place, a savage, concrete jungle. He was glad to be away from the place. He slowed down, suddenly aware that he was speeding.

No, his Chicago was gone, over, ended.